I0002251

# MASTERING SQL QUERIES FOR DATA SCIENCE

Use SQL to Efficiently Query and
Analyze Data for Data Science Projects

## THOMPSON CARTER

**All rights reserved**

No part of this book may be reproduced, distributed, or transmitted in any form or by any means without the prior written permission of the publisher, except in the case of brief quotations embodied in critical reviews and certain other noncommercial uses permitted by copyright law.

# TABLE OF CONTENTS

INTRODUCTION ........................................................................13

WHY SQL MATTERS IN DATA SCIENCE.........................................14

WHAT YOU WILL LEARN ...........................................................15

WHO THIS BOOK IS FOR ...........................................................17

WHY SQL IS KEY TO FUTURE DATA SCIENCE PROJECTS ..........17

STRUCTURE OF THE BOOK..........................................................18

FINAL THOUGHTS.....................................................................20

CHAPTER 1: INTRODUCTION TO SQL AND DATA SCIENCE
....................................................................................................21

INTRODUCTION TO THE ROLE OF SQL IN DATA SCIENCE...........21

THE IMPORTANCE OF DATABASES AND QUERYING IN DATA SCIENCE
WORKFLOWS ...........................................................................22

UNDERSTANDING RELATIONAL DATABASES AND HOW DATA IS STORED
....................................................................................................23

KEY SQL CONCEPTS: TABLES, ROWS, COLUMNS, AND PRIMARY KEYS 24

OVERVIEW OF THE BOOK AND WHAT READERS WILL LEARN..................26

CHAPTER 2: SETTING UP YOUR SQL ENVIRONMENT.........29

INSTALLING SQL TOOLS: MYSQL, POSTGRESQL, AND SQLITE ............29

INTRODUCTION TO CLOUD-BASED DATABASES (AWS, GOOGLE
BIGQUERY)...............................................................................32

CONNECTING TO A DATABASE FROM A PYTHON ENVIRONMENT (USING LIBRARIES LIKE SQLALCHEMY OR PANDAS)..................................................35

BEST PRACTICES FOR DATABASE MANAGEMENT IN DATA SCIENCE PROJECTS.............................................................................................................38

**CHAPTER 3: BASIC SQL QUERYING ...........................................39**

WRITING BASIC SELECT QUERIES TO RETRIEVE DATA............................39

FILTERING DATA WITH WHERE CLAUSES ............................................40

SORTING DATA USING ORDER BY.......................................................42

LIMITING RESULTS WITH LIMIT ..........................................................44

REAL-WORLD EXAMPLE: QUERYING A SALES DATASET TO RETRIEVE SALES DATA FROM A SPECIFIC REGION .................................................45

EXPLANATION:....................................................................................46

**CHAPTER 4: AGGREGATING DATA WITH SQL .........................48**

USING AGGREGATION FUNCTIONS: COUNT, SUM, AVG, MAX, MIN.48

GROUPING DATA WITH GROUP BY.......................................................52

FILTERING AGGREGATED DATA WITH HAVING ...................................53

REAL-WORLD EXAMPLE: ANALYZING WEBSITE TRAFFIC DATA TO CALCULATE TOTAL VISITS PER DAY ......................................................54

**CHAPTER 5: JOINING TABLES: INNER AND OUTER JOINS 58**

UNDERSTANDING THE CONCEPT OF TABLE RELATIONSHIPS....................58

INNER JOIN, LEFT JOIN, RIGHT JOIN, AND FULL OUTER JOIN.....59

JOINING MULTIPLE TABLES TO COMBINE DATA .........................................64

REAL-WORLD EXAMPLE: MERGING CUSTOMER DATA WITH ORDER HISTORY TO ANALYZE PURCHASING BEHAVIOR..........................................65

**CHAPTER 6: ADVANCED JOINS AND SELF JOINS..................68**

UNDERSTANDING SELF JOIN AND ITS USE CASES ....................................68
COMBINING MULTIPLE JOIN TYPES IN ONE QUERY ..................................71
HANDLING COMPLEX DATA RELATIONSHIPS IN DATA SCIENCE PROJECTS..........................................................................................73
REAL-WORLD EXAMPLE: USING SELF JOIN TO FIND THE REPORTING STRUCTURE IN AN EMPLOYEE DATABASE ........................................74

**CHAPTER 7: SUBQUERIES AND NESTED QUERIES...............78**

WRITING SUBQUERIES IN THE SELECT, FROM, WHERE, AND HAVING CLAUSES..........................................................................78
USING SUBQUERIES FOR DATA FILTERING AND AGGREGATION...............83
PERFORMANCE CONSIDERATIONS WHEN USING SUBQUERIES .................84
REAL-WORLD EXAMPLE: FINDING CUSTOMERS WHO MADE PURCHASES ABOVE AVERAGE IN A GIVEN MONTH...........................................85

**CHAPTER 8: WINDOW FUNCTIONS FOR DATA ANALYSIS...88**

INTRODUCTION TO WINDOW FUNCTIONS AND THEIR USE IN DATA SCIENCE.......................................................................................88
USING ROW_NUMBER(), RANK(), DENSE_RANK(), AND NTILE().89
PARTITION BY AND ORDER BY CLAUSES FOR CALCULATING MOVING AVERAGES ..........................................................................92

REAL-WORLD EXAMPLE: ANALYZING STOCK PRICES OVER TIME USING WINDOW FUNCTIONS TO CALCULATE MOVING AVERAGES .....................95

## CHAPTER 9: ADVANCED FILTERING WITH SQL.....................98

USING IN, BETWEEN, LIKE, AND IS NULL FOR COMPLEX FILTERING .............................................................................................................98
REGULAR EXPRESSIONS IN SQL FOR PATTERN MATCHING.................... 102
REAL-WORLD EXAMPLE: FILTERING CUSTOMER DATA TO FIND USERS WHO HAVE SIGNED UP FOR A NEWSLETTER WITHIN THE LAST MONTH ........................................................................................................... 104

## CHAPTER 10: MODIFYING DATA: INSERTING, UPDATING, AND DELETING..........................................................................107

INSERTING NEW DATA INTO A TABLE WITH INSERT INTO .................. 107
UPDATING EXISTING DATA WITH UPDATE............................................. 109
DELETING DATA WITH DELETE AND TRUNCATE................................ 110
REAL-WORLD EXAMPLE: UPDATING CUSTOMER CONTACT INFORMATION IN A DATABASE ..................................................... 113

## CHAPTER 11: CREATING AND MODIFYING TABLES ........... 116

CREATING TABLES USING THE CREATE TABLE STATEMENT............. 116
MODIFYING TABLES WITH ALTER TABLE ............................................. 118
ADDING CONSTRAINTS (PRIMARY KEYS, FOREIGN KEYS, UNIQUE CONSTRAINTS) ............................................................................ 120

REAL-WORLD EXAMPLE: CREATING A TABLE FOR STORING CUSTOMER FEEDBACK IN A DATA SCIENCE PROJECT ..................................................... 123

**CHAPTER 12: INDEXING FOR PERFORMANCE OPTIMIZATION** ......................................................................................... **126**

WHAT INDEXES ARE AND WHY THEY ARE IMPORTANT FOR QUERY PERFORMANCE .............................................................................................. 126
CREATING AND DROPPING INDEXES ............................................................ 127
UNDERSTANDING THE DIFFERENCE BETWEEN CLUSTERED AND NON-CLUSTERED INDEXES .................................................................................... 129
REAL-WORLD EXAMPLE: INDEXING LARGE TRANSACTION TABLES TO SPEED UP QUERY PERFORMANCE .................................................................. 131

**CHAPTER 13: SQL TRANSACTIONS AND DATA INTEGRITY** ............................................................................................................. **135**

UNDERSTANDING THE CONCEPT OF TRANSACTIONS IN SQL ................. 135
USING COMMIT, ROLLBACK, AND SAVEPOINT TO MANAGE DATA CONSISTENCY ................................................................................................... 136
ENSURING DATA INTEGRITY WITH CONSTRAINTS AND NORMALIZATION ............................................................................................................................. 140
REAL-WORLD EXAMPLE: ENSURING DATA INTEGRITY WHEN INSERTING MULTIPLE ROWS INTO A DATABASE ............................................................ 143

**CHAPTER 14: DATA NORMALIZATION AND DENORMALIZATION** ..................................................................................... **146**

THE CONCEPT OF NORMALIZATION AND ITS IMPORTANCE FOR DATABASE DESIGN ........................................................................ 146

THE DIFFERENT NORMAL FORMS (1NF, 2NF, 3NF, ETC.)...................... 147

WHEN AND WHY DENORMALIZATION MIGHT BE NECESSARY FOR DATA SCIENCE .................................................................................. 152

REAL-WORLD EXAMPLE: DESIGNING A CUSTOMER DATA SCHEMA FOR AN E-COMMERCE WEBSITE ........................................................... 153

**CHAPTER 15: SQL PERFORMANCE TUNING ....... 157**

QUERY OPTIMIZATION TECHNIQUES: INDEXING, QUERY REWRITING, AND ANALYZING EXECUTION PLANS ............................................. 157

ANALYZING SLOW QUERIES USING EXPLAIN AND OPTIMIZING THEM ................................................................................................ 161

REAL-WORLD EXAMPLE: OPTIMIZING A QUERY TO FETCH THE MOST POPULAR PRODUCTS FROM A SALES DATASET ........................... 164

**CHAPTER 16: SQL FOR TIME SERIES DATA........... 168**

HANDLING TIME-BASED DATA WITH SQL ................................. 168

USING DATE AND TIME FUNCTIONS IN SQL............................... 169

GROUPING AND AGGREGATING TIME SERIES DATA............................ 171

REAL-WORLD EXAMPLE: ANALYZING WEEKLY SALES TRENDS FOR A PRODUCT CATEGORY .................................................................. 174

**CHAPTER 17: SQL FOR GEOSPATIAL DATA ANALYSIS ........ 178**

INTRODUCTION TO SPATIAL DATA TYPES IN SQL .................................. 178

USING SQL TO QUERY AND ANALYZE GEOSPATIAL DATA .................... 181

REAL-WORLD EXAMPLE: ANALYZING CUSTOMER LOCATIONS AND
PERFORMING PROXIMITY ANALYSIS TO IDENTIFY SERVICE GAPS ....... 184

**CHAPTER 18: HANDLING MISSING DATA WITH SQL .......... 188**

TECHNIQUES FOR HANDLING MISSING OR NULL VALUES IN SQL
QUERIES.................................................................................... 188

REAL-WORLD EXAMPLE: CLEANING CUSTOMER DATA BY REPLACING
MISSING CONTACT INFORMATION ................................................. 192

**CHAPTER 19: ADVANCED DATA AGGREGATION
TECHNIQUES............................................................................ 197**

USING GROUP_CONCAT AND STRING_AGG FOR COMBINING
MULTIPLE ROWS INTO A SINGLE STRING ....................................... 197

PIVOTING DATA IN SQL USING CONDITIONAL AGGREGATION ............ 200

REAL-WORLD EXAMPLE: AGGREGATING SURVEY RESPONSES BY
GROUPING DATA INTO CATEGORIES ............................................. 202

**CHAPTER 20: SQL FOR DATA WAREHOUSING ..................... 207**

INTRODUCTION TO DATA WAREHOUSING CONCEPTS AND SCHEMA
DESIGN..................................................................................... 207

USING SQL TO PERFORM EXTRACT, TRANSFORM, LOAD (ETL)
OPERATIONS ............................................................................. 211

REAL-WORLD EXAMPLE: BUILDING A DATA WAREHOUSE FOR SALES
REPORTING ............................................................................... 213

## CHAPTER 21: SQL FOR DATA SCIENCE PROJECTS ............... 218

INTEGRATING SQL WITH DATA SCIENCE WORKFLOWS .......................... 218
USING SQL WITH PYTHON AND R FOR DATA MANIPULATION AND
ANALYSIS ................................................................................................ 220
REAL-WORLD EXAMPLE: QUERYING A DATABASE TO PREPARE DATA
FOR MACHINE LEARNING MODELS ............................................................ 225

## CHAPTER 22: INTEGRATING SQL WITH MACHINE
## LEARNING WORKFLOWS ......................................................... 229

USING SQL TO PREPARE DATASETS FOR MACHINE LEARNING ............. 229
EXTRACTING TRAINING DATA USING COMPLEX SQL QUERIES ............ 233
REAL-WORLD EXAMPLE: PREPARING CUSTOMER BEHAVIOR DATA FOR
A MACHINE LEARNING MODEL IN A MARKETING CAMPAIGN ............... 235

## CHAPTER 23: ADVANCED SQL FOR BIG DATA ...................... 241

INTRODUCTION TO SQL FOR BIG DATA PLATFORMS .............................. 241
OPTIMIZING QUERIES FOR LARGE-SCALE DATASETS ............................ 245
REAL-WORLD EXAMPLE: RUNNING SQL QUERIES ON A MASSIVE
DATASET TO ANALYZE USER BEHAVIOR ACROSS MULTIPLE REGIONS
................................................................................................................ 247

## CHAPTER 24: USING SQL FOR DATA VISUALIZATION ........ 251

QUERYING DATA FOR USE IN VISUALIZATIONS ..................................... 251
INTEGRATING SQL WITH DATA VISUALIZATION TOOLS ........................ 254

REAL-WORLD EXAMPLE: QUERYING AND VISUALIZING SALES DATA
USING TABLEAU ......................................................................................... 259

## CHAPTER 25: TROUBLESHOOTING AND DEBUGGING SQL QUERIES ................................................................................................. 262

COMMON ERRORS IN SQL QUERIES AND HOW TO FIX THEM ................ 262
DEBUGGING TECHNIQUES TO IDENTIFY ISSUES WITH SQL QUERIES ... 265
REAL-WORLD EXAMPLE: TROUBLESHOOTING A QUERY THAT JOINS
MULTIPLE TABLES AND RETURNS INCORRECT RESULTS ........................ 268

## CHAPTER 26: BUILDING REUSABLE SQL QUERIES FOR DATA SCIENCE ......................................................................................... 272

WRITING EFFICIENT, REUSABLE SQL QUERIES FOR REPORTING AND
DATA ANALYSIS ......................................................................................... 272
CREATING VIEWS AND STORED PROCEDURES TO ENCAPSULATE SQL
LOGIC ......................................................................................................... 275
REAL-WORLD EXAMPLE: CREATING A SET OF VIEWS TO REGULARLY
MONITOR BUSINESS KPIS IN AN ORGANIZATION ..................................... 278

## CHAPTER 27: THE FUTURE OF SQL AND DATA SCIENCE .282

THE EVOLVING ROLE OF SQL IN DATA SCIENCE AS NEW TECHNOLOGIES
EMERGE ...................................................................................................... 282
TRENDS IN SQL QUERY OPTIMIZATION AND BIG DATA .......................... 284
THE IMPORTANCE OF MASTERING SQL FOR FUTURE DATA SCIENCE
PROJECTS .................................................................................................... 287

FINAL THOUGHTS ON BECOMING AN EXPERT SQL USER IN DATA SCIENCE ................................................................................................. 288

# Introduction

**Introduction to** *Mastering SQL Queries for Data Science*

Data science has evolved into one of the most sought-after fields in the modern world, fueling breakthroughs in industries ranging from healthcare and finance to technology and entertainment. With the growing reliance on data-driven decisions, the ability to **effectively query** and **analyze data** has become indispensable. While there are many tools and techniques available for data scientists, **SQL (Structured Query Language)** remains the foundation of working with relational databases, a cornerstone of data manipulation and analysis.

**SQL** is the universal language used to manage and retrieve data stored in relational databases. Whether you're dealing with small datasets or massive volumes of big data, SQL provides the framework for extracting, transforming, and querying data in ways that are essential for effective analysis. Despite its age, SQL is not only still relevant but is continually evolving, making it an essential skill for any aspiring or experienced data scientist.

This book, ***Mastering SQL Queries for Data Science***, is designed to guide you through the essential SQL techniques required for efficient data querying and analysis. The book is structured to help you develop both foundational knowledge and practical skills, with the end goal of becoming proficient in writing and optimizing SQL queries for complex data science projects. Whether you're working with traditional relational databases, big data platforms, or integrating SQL into machine learning workflows, this book will equip you with the tools needed to succeed.

---

## Why SQL Matters in Data Science

Data science is all about leveraging data to gain insights, predict future trends, and make better decisions. The sheer amount of data we generate every day has given rise to **big data** technologies, cloud computing platforms, and machine learning tools. However, no matter how advanced these tools get, SQL remains central to accessing and querying data.

SQL empowers data scientists to:

- **Access and manipulate data**: SQL allows data scientists to write queries to retrieve the data they need from a database, filter it, and join it with other data sources to build the dataset they will analyze.
- **Clean and transform data**: Data is rarely in the right format for analysis. SQL provides the functions and operations to clean, normalize, and transform data into the form needed for downstream tasks like machine learning, statistical analysis, and business intelligence.

- **Aggregate and summarize data**: SQL's powerful aggregation capabilities enable data scientists to compute sums, averages, counts, and more—operations that are vital in analyzing trends, comparing metrics, and summarizing findings.
- **Work with complex datasets**: In real-world data science projects, data often exists in multiple tables. SQL's ability to handle **joins**, **subqueries**, and **aggregations** makes it indispensable for working with relational datasets.

## What You Will Learn

This book is designed to be both comprehensive and practical. You will learn how to master SQL queries step-by-step, from the basics to advanced techniques that are relevant to the work you will encounter in data science projects. Each chapter is designed to introduce you to essential SQL concepts and provide you with the skills to apply them directly in the context of data science.

*Key Topics Covered:*

1. **Foundational SQL**: We'll begin with the basics, including writing simple SELECT queries to retrieve data, filtering data with WHERE clauses, and sorting results with ORDER BY.

2. **Working with Joins and Aggregations**: You'll learn how to work with multiple tables using joins and how to aggregate data with SQL's powerful functions like SUM, COUNT, and AVG.

3. **Advanced SQL Techniques**: We will cover advanced topics such as **subqueries**, **window functions**, and **common table expressions (CTEs)**, all of which are essential for complex data manipulation and analysis.

4. **SQL for Data Science Projects**: Special focus will be placed on how SQL integrates with data science workflows, including how to query data for machine learning, how to prepare data for predictive modeling, and how to leverage SQL for big data projects.

5. **SQL Optimization and Best Practices**: As datasets grow larger, the need for optimizing SQL queries becomes critical. We'll explore best practices for writing efficient SQL queries and techniques for improving query performance, including the use of **indexes**, **query optimization**, and **parallel processing**.

Through **real-world examples**, you'll see how SQL can be used to solve common data science problems, including preparing datasets for analysis, working with time series data, aggregating sales performance, and predicting customer churn.

## Who This Book Is For

This book is for anyone interested in mastering SQL in the context of data science, regardless of your background. Whether you're just getting started in data science or looking to enhance your existing skills, you will find value in this book. It is particularly suited for:

- **Aspiring data scientists** who need a comprehensive understanding of SQL to work with databases and big data platforms.
- **Business analysts** who need to use SQL to extract and analyze data for reports and decision-making.
- **Machine learning practitioners** who want to understand how to use SQL for data preprocessing and integration in machine learning pipelines.
- **Data engineers** who want to learn best practices for designing and managing SQL-based data systems.

---

## Why SQL is Key to Future Data Science Projects

As data science continues to evolve, SQL remains a critical tool in the data scientist's toolkit. Here's why:

1. **SQL Powers Big Data and Cloud Databases**: Modern platforms like **Google BigQuery**, **Amazon Redshift**, and

**Apache Hive** rely on SQL for querying massive datasets stored in the cloud. These platforms combine the scalability of cloud computing with the simplicity of SQL, making them essential for big data analysis.

2. **SQL Supports Advanced Analytics and Machine Learning**: Many machine learning frameworks (like **BigQuery ML** or **SQL Server Machine Learning Services**) allow you to build machine learning models directly within SQL, making it even more important to understand how to work with SQL in these contexts.

3. **SQL is Universal**: Despite the rise of new technologies and tools, SQL remains one of the most widely used languages in data management. Its standardized nature means that learning SQL allows you to work with virtually any relational database, from **MySQL** to **PostgreSQL** to **SQL Server**.

By mastering SQL, you will be equipped to work with both small datasets and large, distributed systems, whether your focus is on **data analysis**, **machine learning**, or **big data analytics**.

## Structure of the Book

This book is divided into 27 chapters, with each chapter focusing on a specific area of SQL relevant to data science. The chapters progress logically, starting with foundational concepts and building up to more advanced topics. You'll find practical examples, real-world use cases, and hands-on exercises to reinforce the concepts presented.

The structure of the book is as follows:

1. **Chapter 1: Introduction to SQL and Data Science** – Overview of SQL's importance in data science.
2. **Chapter 2: Setting Up Your SQL Environment** – How to install and configure SQL tools.
3. **Chapter 3: Basic SQL Querying** – Writing simple queries to retrieve data.
4. **Chapter 4: Aggregating Data with SQL** – Using SQL to perform calculations like sums and averages.
5. **Chapter 5: Joining Tables** – Combining data from multiple tables with JOINs.
6. **Chapter 6: Advanced Joins and Subqueries** – Using complex joins and subqueries for advanced analysis.
7. **Chapter 7: SQL Optimization** – Best practices for optimizing SQL queries for performance.

… and much more, covering topics like **data visualization, time-series data**, **data lakes**, and **integration with machine learning**.

## Final Thoughts

By the end of this book, you will not only be proficient in writing SQL queries but also equipped with the skills to apply them in a **data science** context, optimizing data workflows and solving real-world problems. Whether you're analyzing business metrics, cleaning and preparing data for machine learning models, or querying big data, mastering SQL will give you the tools to make powerful, data-driven decisions.

Welcome to the journey of becoming a **master of SQL** for **data science**. Let's get started!

# Chapter 1: Introduction to SQL and Data Science

## Introduction to the Role of SQL in Data Science

In the modern world of data science, the ability to query, manipulate, and analyze data is essential for uncovering insights that drive decision-making. While data science involves many complex tools and techniques, **SQL** (Structured Query Language) remains one of the most important and foundational skills for data scientists. SQL allows data scientists to interact with relational databases—one of the primary storage methods for structured data. Whether you're working with large datasets, analyzing user behavior, or performing data cleaning, SQL is often the tool that will help you access, query, and manipulate the data you need.

SQL enables you to perform tasks ranging from simple data retrieval to complex transformations and aggregations. In fact, SQL is so ingrained in the data science process that it is often the first step in any data analysis workflow. Before diving into machine learning models or advanced analytics, data scientists often spend significant time querying databases to ensure they have the clean, relevant, and structured data required for analysis.

This book will guide you through the entire process of mastering SQL, specifically in the context of data science projects. Whether you're a beginner or an experienced data analyst, you will gain the skills necessary to efficiently query, manipulate, and analyze data from relational databases.

## The Importance of Databases and Querying in Data Science Workflows

At the heart of every data-driven organization lies a vast array of databases that store the data needed to run the business. These databases are typically relational, meaning that data is organized into tables that can be linked together through **relationships**. SQL is the primary language used to interact with these databases. As data scientists, one of our most common tasks is to extract useful data from these relational databases and bring it into an environment where we can analyze it, visualize it, and model it.

In a typical data science workflow, **data acquisition** is one of the first and most crucial steps. This is where SQL comes into play—allowing you to write **queries** to extract, filter, and transform data from relational databases. Once the relevant data has been extracted, it is typically cleaned, processed, and transformed for analysis. The ability to query databases efficiently helps ensure that data scientists can work quickly and efficiently, accessing only the most relevant information.

Additionally, databases serve as the backbone for data storage in large-scale applications, making it imperative for data scientists to understand how to query databases efficiently. Whether you're working with business data (sales, customer behavior), scientific data (experiment results, genomic data), or internet data (website traffic, user activity logs), understanding how to use SQL is key to navigating and extracting the insights hidden within that data.

## Understanding Relational Databases and How Data is Stored

**Relational databases** are structured databases where data is stored in tables. Each table is a collection of related data, organized into rows and columns. Relational databases are the most common type of database in use today, due to their simplicity, flexibility, and scalability.

Here's a breakdown of key concepts in relational databases:

- **Tables**: A table is a collection of related data stored in rows and columns. Each table stores data about a specific type of entity (e.g., customers, products, orders). In SQL, the table is the main unit of storage.
- **Rows**: A row (also known as a record or tuple) represents a single data entry in a table. Each row contains information about an entity, such as a customer's name, address, or transaction history.
- **Columns**: A column (also known as a field or attribute) represents a particular attribute or property of the entity

stored in the table. For example, in a customer table, columns might include **CustomerID**, **Name**, **Email**, and **Phone**.

- **Primary Keys**: A primary key is a unique identifier for a row within a table. It ensures that each row can be uniquely identified, and no two rows in the table can have the same primary key value. In most databases, the **CustomerID** in a customer table would be the primary key because each customer must have a unique ID.

- **Foreign Keys**: Foreign keys are used to link one table to another. A foreign key in one table refers to the primary key of another table, creating a relationship between the two. For example, an **Orders** table might have a foreign key that links to the **CustomerID** from the **Customers** table, establishing a relationship between orders and customers.

Relational databases make it easy to store, organize, and manage large amounts of structured data. By understanding the core concepts of tables, rows, columns, and primary keys, data scientists can start querying databases to extract the data they need for analysis.

## Key SQL Concepts: Tables, Rows, Columns, and Primary Keys

When working with SQL, you'll encounter several core concepts that are essential for querying and manipulating data. Below, we provide an introduction to the fundamental concepts that form the foundation of SQL queries:

## 1. Tables

As mentioned, tables are the central units of data storage in relational databases. A table consists of rows and columns, and each column represents an attribute of the data, while each row represents a single record. For example, the **Customers** table might have columns for **CustomerID**, **Name**, **Email**, and **Phone**.

## 2. Rows

Each row in a table contains data for one entity. For example, one row in the **Customers** table might contain information about a specific customer: their ID, name, email address, and phone number. Rows can be inserted, updated, or deleted using SQL queries.

## 3. Columns

Columns define the types of data that will be stored in the table. For example, the **Email** column in a **Customers** table will store email addresses for each customer. Columns can have different data types, such as integers, strings, dates, and more.

## 4. Primary Keys

A primary key is a unique identifier for a row in a table. It ensures that each row can be uniquely identified, and no two rows can have the same primary key value. Primary keys are essential for maintaining data integrity and for establishing relationships between tables. For instance, a **CustomerID** column might be the primary key in the **Customers** table, ensuring each customer has a unique identifier.

## Overview of the Book and What Readers Will Learn

This book is designed to guide you step-by-step through the essential skills you need to master SQL for data science projects. Whether you're new to databases or already familiar with SQL, this book provides you with a solid foundation and practical, real-world examples to ensure you can apply what you've learned.

*What You Will Learn in This Book:*

- **Fundamental SQL concepts** such as tables, rows, columns, primary keys, and relationships between tables.
- **Basic to advanced querying techniques**, including data retrieval, filtering, sorting, and grouping.
- **How to join tables** and combine data from multiple sources using various types of joins.
- **Data aggregation** and summary techniques to extract meaningful insights from large datasets.
- **Working with time-series data** and how to analyze trends over time using SQL.
- **Best practices for optimizing queries** to improve performance when dealing with large datasets.

- **How to handle missing data**, clean datasets, and prepare data for analysis.
- **Advanced topics** such as window functions, subqueries, and the integration of SQL with data science workflows.

***Real-World Examples:***

Throughout the book, you will encounter real-world examples drawn from various fields of data science. For instance, we'll look at querying sales data to identify trends in customer behavior, or analyzing website traffic data to understand which pages attract the most visitors. By the end of the book, you'll have a robust understanding of how SQL can be used to power data science projects, from data acquisition and cleaning to analysis and visualization.

This book is not just about learning SQL syntax; it's about learning how to use SQL to solve real data problems and get meaningful insights. With the skills you'll gain here, you'll be well on your way to becoming proficient in SQL and ready to tackle any data science project that comes your way.

In summary, **Chapter 1** serves as an introduction to SQL, providing the foundational knowledge necessary for mastering SQL in the context of data science. You'll learn about relational databases, the core concepts of SQL, and the importance of querying in data science workflows. As we progress through this book, we'll delve deeper into SQL's capabilities, ultimately empowering you to use SQL to efficiently query and analyze data for data science projects.

# Chapter 2: Setting Up Your SQL Environment

## Installing SQL Tools: MySQL, PostgreSQL, and SQLite

Before you can start querying and analyzing data with SQL, you need to install and set up an appropriate SQL environment. There are several widely used relational database management systems (RDBMS) you can choose from, depending on your needs. Below is an introduction to the installation and setup of three popular SQL tools: **MySQL**, **PostgreSQL**, and **SQLite**.

### *1. MySQL*

MySQL is one of the most widely used relational databases, known for its speed and reliability. It's ideal for managing large-scale databases and supports various platforms, including Linux, Windows, and macOS.

- **Installation Steps**:
    1. **Download MySQL Installer**: Visit the official MySQL website and download the installer for your operating system (Windows, macOS, or Linux). The installer is available at MySQL Downloads.
    2. **Run the Installer**: The installer will guide you through the process, allowing you to choose

additional components like MySQL Workbench for managing your databases visually.

3. **Configure MySQL**: During installation, you'll be asked to configure MySQL, such as setting up the root password and choosing a default database port (usually 3306).

4. **Start MySQL Server**: After installation, launch MySQL Workbench or use the MySQL command line to connect to the server and begin creating databases.

### 2. PostgreSQL

PostgreSQL is an open-source relational database that emphasizes extensibility and SQL compliance. It's well-suited for complex queries, analytics, and transactional systems.

- **Installation Steps**:
    1. **Download PostgreSQL**: Visit the official PostgreSQL website and download the installer for your platform (Windows, macOS, or Linux). You can find the download at PostgreSQL Downloads.
    2. **Run the Installer**: After downloading, run the installer and follow the prompts to install PostgreSQL. The setup wizard will also install **pgAdmin**, a GUI for managing PostgreSQL databases.

3. **Set up PostgreSQL**: You'll be prompted to set the PostgreSQL superuser password during installation. Choose a password that you'll remember, as it's required to access the database.

4. **Connect to PostgreSQL**: After installation, open **pgAdmin** or use the command line to interact with the PostgreSQL database server.

### 3. SQLite

SQLite is a serverless, self-contained database engine that is ideal for lightweight, local, and embedded applications. Unlike MySQL and PostgreSQL, SQLite does not require a separate server process.

- **Installation Steps**:
    1. **Download SQLite**: SQLite is extremely lightweight and does not require a traditional installation process. You can download the binary directly from the official SQLite website at SQLite Downloads.
    2. **Install SQLite**: After downloading, extract the file and place it in a directory of your choice. Add the directory to your system's PATH environment variable to use SQLite from the command line.
    3. **Use SQLite**: You can start using SQLite directly by running the sqlite3 command in the terminal, followed by the database file you want to access or create.

Each of these databases has its unique strengths, so you should select the one that best fits your project's needs. MySQL and PostgreSQL are typically used in large-scale production systems, while SQLite is great for smaller, embedded applications and local testing.

## Introduction to Cloud-Based Databases (AWS, Google BigQuery)

With the increasing volume of data, cloud-based databases have become an essential tool in modern data science. They provide scalable, secure, and cost-efficient solutions for storing and querying large datasets. Below are some of the leading cloud-based databases that data scientists use for data science projects: **Amazon Web Services (AWS)** and **Google BigQuery**.

### 1. Amazon Web Services (AWS) – RDS

Amazon RDS (Relational Database Service) makes it easier to set up, operate, and scale a relational database in the cloud. AWS RDS supports multiple database engines, including MySQL, PostgreSQL, Oracle, and SQL Server.

- **Getting Started with AWS RDS**:
    1. **Sign up for an AWS account**: If you don't already have an AWS account, you'll need to create one at AWS.

2. **Create an RDS Instance**: Once logged into the AWS console, navigate to the RDS section and launch a new RDS instance. You'll need to select the database engine (e.g., MySQL, PostgreSQL), specify instance details (such as instance type and storage), and configure security settings.

3. **Connect to Your Database**: After creating the RDS instance, you can connect to it using any SQL client (e.g., MySQL Workbench, pgAdmin) by specifying the endpoint and using the credentials you set during setup.

- **Advantages of AWS RDS**:
  - o Fully managed and scalable database solution.
  - o High availability and automated backups.
  - o Integration with other AWS services like S3, Lambda, and Redshift.

## 2. Google BigQuery

Google BigQuery is a fully-managed, serverless data warehouse that is designed to analyze large datasets quickly. It supports SQL queries and integrates seamlessly with other Google Cloud services, making it a powerful tool for data science.

- **Getting Started with Google BigQuery**:

1. **Sign up for Google Cloud**: If you don't have an account, you can sign up for Google Cloud at Google Cloud.

2. **Create a BigQuery Project**: After signing in, navigate to BigQuery from the Google Cloud Console. You can create a new project or select an existing one to begin using BigQuery.

3. **Upload Data to BigQuery**: You can upload datasets from Google Cloud Storage or other sources, and BigQuery supports file formats like CSV, JSON, and Parquet.

4. **Run SQL Queries**: Once the data is uploaded, you can begin querying it using SQL within the BigQuery Console. BigQuery also integrates with tools like **Data Studio** for data visualization.

- **Advantages of Google BigQuery**:
  - Extremely fast and scalable, especially for large datasets.
  - No server management required; fully serverless architecture.
  - Integration with various Google Cloud tools, such as AI and machine learning APIs.

# Connecting to a Database from a Python Environment (Using Libraries like SQLAlchemy or Pandas)

Data scientists often need to interact with databases directly from their Python environment. Fortunately, there are several libraries that facilitate this process, making it easier to query databases, manipulate data, and integrate the results into your data science projects.

## *1. SQLAlchemy*

SQLAlchemy is a powerful and flexible Python library that provides an **Object Relational Mapping (ORM)** layer and allows you to query databases using SQL. It supports a wide range of database backends, including MySQL, PostgreSQL, and SQLite.

- **Installing SQLAlchemy**: To install SQLAlchemy, use the following pip command:

  ```bash
  Copy
  pip install sqlalchemy
  ```

- **Connecting to a Database**: Here's an example of how to connect to a MySQL database using SQLAlchemy:

  ```python
  Copy
  from sqlalchemy import create_engine
  ```

```
# Replace with your database credentials
DATABASE_URL                                    =
"mysql+pymysql://user:password@localhost/mydatabase"

# Create a database engine
engine = create_engine(DATABASE_URL)

# Connect to the database
connection = engine.connect()
```

- **Querying the Database**: After establishing the connection, you can use SQLAlchemy to write queries:

```python
python
Copy
result = connection.execute("SELECT * FROM customers")
for row in result:
    print(row)
```

## 2. Pandas

Pandas is a widely-used library for data analysis in Python, and it offers convenient methods for querying SQL databases and importing the data into DataFrame structures for easy manipulation.

- **Installing Pandas**: To install Pandas, use the following pip command:

```bash
bash
Copy
```

pip install pandas

- **Connecting to a Database**: Here's an example of connecting to a PostgreSQL database using Pandas:

```python
Copy
import pandas as pd
import psycopg2

# Establish a connection to the database
conn = psycopg2.connect("dbname=test user=postgres password=secret")

# Write a SQL query
query = "SELECT * FROM sales"

# Load the data into a Pandas DataFrame
df = pd.read_sql(query, conn)

# Close the connection
conn.close()

# View the first few rows of data
print(df.head())
```

- **Querying the Database**: Once the data is loaded into a DataFrame, you can use all of Pandas' data manipulation tools to analyze and process the data.

## Best Practices for Database Management in Data Science Projects

Effective database management is essential for ensuring the quality, scalability, and performance of your data science projects. Here are some best practices to follow when working with databases in data science:

### *1. Organize and Structure Data:*

- Normalize your data when designing relational schemas to reduce redundancy and ensure data consistency.
- Use meaningful table and column names to make queries easy to read and understand.
- Use appropriate data types for each column (e.g., use INT for integers, VARCHAR for text, DATE for date fields).

### *2. Optimize Queries for Performance:*

- Write efficient SQL queries by avoiding unnecessary joins, subqueries, and nested

# Chapter 3: Basic SQL Querying

In this chapter, we'll dive into the basics of SQL querying, focusing on fundamental techniques that will enable you to retrieve and filter data effectively from relational databases. By the end of this chapter, you will be comfortable writing simple SQL queries, filtering and sorting data, and limiting the number of results you retrieve.

## Writing Basic SELECT Queries to Retrieve Data

The **SELECT** statement is the most basic and essential SQL command for retrieving data from a database. It allows you to specify which columns of data you want to pull from a table.

### *Syntax:*

```sql
Copy
SELECT column1, column2, ..., columnN
FROM table_name;
```

- **SELECT**: Specifies the columns you want to retrieve.
- **FROM**: Specifies the table from which to retrieve the data.

### *Example 1:*

Let's say we have a **Customers** table, and we want to retrieve the customer names and email addresses.

```sql
```

Copy

SELECT customer_name, email

FROM Customers;

This query will return all rows from the **Customers** table, showing only the **customer_name** and **email** columns.

### *Example 2:*

If you want to retrieve all columns from a table, you can use the * wildcard, which represents all columns:

sql

Copy

SELECT *

FROM Customers;

This will return every column for every row in the **Customers** table.

---

## Filtering Data with WHERE Clauses

The **WHERE** clause allows you to filter data based on specified conditions. You can use various operators to filter your data, including =, >, <, >=, <=, <> (not equal), BETWEEN, IN, LIKE, and IS NULL.

### *Syntax:*

sql

Copy

SELECT column1, column2, ...

FROM table_name

WHERE condition;

### *Common operators in WHERE clauses:*

- =: Equal to
- >: Greater than
- <: Less than
- **BETWEEN**: Within a range of values
- **IN**: Match one of a list of values
- **LIKE**: Pattern matching (often used with %)
- **IS NULL**: Check for null values

### *Example 1:*

To filter data to retrieve customers from a specific city, say "New York," you would write:

sql

Copy

```
SELECT customer_name, email
FROM Customers
WHERE city = 'New York';
```

This query will return only the customers who reside in **New York**.

### *Example 2:*

To retrieve sales transactions where the sales amount is greater than $1000, you can use the > operator:

sql

Copy

```
SELECT transaction_id, amount
FROM Sales
WHERE amount > 1000;
```

This query will return all transactions with amounts greater than $1000.

### Example 3:

To retrieve data for a set of values, such as customers from specific cities, you can use the IN operator:

```
sql
Copy
SELECT customer_name, email
FROM Customers
WHERE city IN ('New York', 'Los Angeles', 'Chicago');
```

This query retrieves customers who live in **New York**, **Los Angeles**, or **Chicago**.

---

## Sorting Data Using ORDER BY

The **ORDER BY** clause allows you to sort the result set of your query based on one or more columns. By default, the results will be sorted in **ascending order** (ASC), but you can also specify **descending order** (DESC).

### Syntax:
sql

Copy

```
SELECT column1, column2, ...
FROM table_name
ORDER BY column1 [ASC|DESC], column2 [ASC|DESC], ...;
```

## *Example 1:*

If you want to retrieve all customers sorted by their **customer_name** in ascending order:

sql

Copy

```
SELECT customer_name, email
FROM Customers
ORDER BY customer_name ASC;
```

This will return customers sorted alphabetically by their name in ascending order.

## *Example 2:*

To sort sales data by **amount** in descending order (highest sales first):

sql

Copy

```
SELECT transaction_id, amount
FROM Sales
ORDER BY amount DESC;
```

This query will list the transactions starting from the highest sale amount.

## *Example 3:*

You can also sort by multiple columns. For instance, if you want to sort customers first by **city** (alphabetically) and then by **customer_name** (alphabetically):

sql
Copy
SELECT customer_name, city, email
FROM Customers
ORDER BY city ASC, customer_name ASC;

This will first sort by **city**, and within each city, it will sort customers by **name**.

---

## Limiting Results with LIMIT

The **LIMIT** clause restricts the number of rows returned by the query. This is particularly useful when working with large datasets or when you only need a sample of the data for analysis.

*Syntax:*
sql
Copy
SELECT column1, column2, ...
FROM table_name
LIMIT number;

*Example 1:*
To retrieve only the top 5 customers from the **Customers** table:

sql

Copy

```
SELECT customer_name, email
FROM Customers
LIMIT 5;
```

This query will return the first 5 rows of the result set.

### *Example 2:*

You can also use **LIMIT** with **ORDER BY** to retrieve the top n records sorted by a specific column. For instance, to retrieve the top 10 highest sales amounts:

sql

Copy

```
SELECT transaction_id, amount
FROM Sales
ORDER BY amount DESC
LIMIT 10;
```

This will return the top 10 sales transactions, sorted from the highest to the lowest amount.

---

## Real-World Example: Querying a Sales Dataset to Retrieve Sales Data from a Specific Region

Let's now combine all of these concepts into a real-world example using a hypothetical **Sales** dataset. Suppose you have a **Sales** table with the following columns:

45

- **transaction_id**: Unique identifier for each transaction.
- **sales_amount**: Amount of the sale.
- **region**: Region where the sale occurred.
- **sales_date**: Date of the sale.

You want to retrieve the sales data for a specific region, say **"East"**, and filter the data to include only transactions that are greater than $500. Additionally, you want to sort the results by the **sales_amount** in descending order, and limit the result to the top 10 sales.

Here's how you would write the SQL query:

```sql
Copy
SELECT transaction_id, sales_amount, region, sales_date
FROM Sales
WHERE region = 'East' AND sales_amount > 500
ORDER BY sales_amount DESC
LIMIT 10;
```

## Explanation:

- **SELECT**: Retrieves the **transaction_id**, **sales_amount**, **region**, and **sales_date** columns from the **Sales** table.
- **WHERE**: Filters the data to include only records where the **region** is **'East'** and the **sales_amount** is greater than 500.
- **ORDER BY**: Sorts the results by **sales_amount** in descending order, showing the highest sales first.

- **LIMIT**: Restricts the result set to the top 10 rows.

---

In this chapter, we covered the basics of SQL querying: retrieving data with **SELECT** statements, filtering data with **WHERE** clauses, sorting data with **ORDER BY**, and limiting the number of results using **LIMIT**. These are foundational skills that every data scientist must master to work efficiently with SQL databases.

Through the real-world example of querying a sales dataset, you've seen how to combine these techniques to write meaningful queries that allow you to extract relevant data and analyze it effectively. As you move forward, you'll build on these concepts, learning more advanced techniques for working with SQL in data science projects.

In the next chapter, we will explore **aggregating data**, which will enable you to summarize and analyze data at a higher level, turning raw data into actionable insights.

# Chapter 4: Aggregating Data with SQL

In this chapter, we'll explore how to summarize and analyze large datasets using SQL's aggregation functions. Aggregating data allows you to derive meaningful insights from raw data by calculating metrics like totals, averages, maximums, and minimums. You'll also learn how to group data by specific columns and filter aggregated data to further refine your analysis.

## Using Aggregation Functions: COUNT, SUM, AVG, MAX, MIN

SQL provides several powerful aggregation functions that allow you to summarize data and perform calculations on numeric columns. These functions can be used to calculate totals, averages, counts, and more, depending on your analysis needs.

### 1. COUNT()

The COUNT() function returns the number of rows that match a specified condition or the total number of rows in a table.

- **Syntax**:

```sql
Copy
SELECT COUNT(column_name)
FROM table_name;
```

- **Example**: To count the total number of customers in the **Customers** table:

sql
Copy
SELECT COUNT(*)
FROM Customers;

This query will return the total number of rows (customers) in the **Customers** table.

## 2. SUM()

The SUM() function calculates the total sum of a numeric column.

- **Syntax**:

sql
Copy
SELECT SUM(column_name)
FROM table_name;

- **Example**: To calculate the total sales amount in the **Sales** table:

sql
Copy
SELECT SUM(sales_amount)
FROM Sales;

This query will return the total value of **sales_amount** across all rows in the **Sales** table.

## 3. AVG()

The AVG() function calculates the average value of a numeric column.

- **Syntax**:

```sql
Copy
SELECT AVG(column_name)
FROM table_name;
```

- **Example**: To calculate the average sales amount in the **Sales** table:

```sql
Copy
SELECT AVG(sales_amount)
FROM Sales;
```

This query will return the average **sales_amount** across all transactions in the **Sales** table.

## 4. MAX()

The MAX() function returns the highest value in a numeric column.

- **Syntax**:

```sql
Copy
SELECT MAX(column_name)
FROM table_name;
```

- **Example**: To find the highest sales amount in the **Sales** table:

sql

Copy

SELECT MAX(sales_amount)

FROM Sales;

This query will return the maximum **sales_amount** recorded in the **Sales** table.

## 5. MIN()

The MIN() function returns the lowest value in a numeric column.

- **Syntax**:

sql

Copy

SELECT MIN(column_name)

FROM table_name;

- **Example**: To find the smallest sales amount in the **Sales** table:

sql

Copy

SELECT MIN(sales_amount)

FROM Sales;

This query will return the minimum **sales_amount** recorded in the **Sales** table.

## Grouping Data with GROUP BY

The **GROUP BY** clause is used in conjunction with aggregation functions to group rows that share a common value into summary rows. It allows you to calculate aggregates for each group of data, such as total sales by region or average transaction amount by customer.

### *Syntax:*

sql

Copy

```
SELECT column_name, AGGREGATE_FUNCTION(column_name)
FROM table_name
GROUP BY column_name;
```

- **Example**: To calculate the total sales per region, you can group the sales data by the **region** column:

sql

Copy

```
SELECT region, SUM(sales_amount)
FROM Sales
GROUP BY region;
```

This query will return the total sales amount for each **region** in the **Sales** table.

### *Example with Multiple Columns:*

You can group data by multiple columns. For example, if you want to calculate the total sales amount per region and per month, you would group by both **region** and **sales_date** (converted to month):

sql
Copy
```
SELECT region, EXTRACT(MONTH FROM sales_date) AS month, SUM(sales_amount)
FROM Sales
GROUP BY region, month;
```
This query will return the total sales for each region for each month, grouping the data by **region** and **month**.

## Filtering Aggregated Data with HAVING

While the **WHERE** clause filters data before aggregation, the **HAVING** clause filters the results after aggregation has been performed. This is useful when you want to apply conditions to the aggregated results, such as only showing regions with total sales greater than a specific amount.

### *Syntax:*
sql
Copy
```
SELECT column_name, AGGREGATE_FUNCTION(column_name)
FROM table_name
GROUP BY column_name
```

HAVING condition;

- **Example**: If you want to find regions where the total sales amount is greater than $5000, you can use the **HAVING** clause:

sql

Copy

```
SELECT region, SUM(sales_amount)
FROM Sales
GROUP BY region
HAVING SUM(sales_amount) > 5000;
```

This query will return only those regions where the total **sales_amount** exceeds $5000.

---

## Real-World Example: Analyzing Website Traffic Data to Calculate Total Visits Per Day

Let's apply these concepts to a real-world scenario. Suppose you have a **WebsiteTraffic** table with the following columns:

- **visit_id**: Unique identifier for each visit.
- **visit_date**: The date and time of the visit.
- **visitor_ip**: The IP address of the visitor.

You want to calculate the total number of visits per day on your website.

## *Step-by-Step Query:*

1. We'll use the **COUNT()** function to count the number of visits for each day.
2. We'll use the **GROUP BY** clause to group the data by the **visit_date** column (after converting it to a date format).
3. We'll sort the results by date using **ORDER BY**.

sql
Copy

```
SELECT DATE(visit_date) AS visit_day, COUNT(*) AS total_visits
FROM WebsiteTraffic
GROUP BY visit_day
ORDER BY visit_day;
```

## *Explanation:*

- **DATE(visit_date)**: The DATE() function is used to extract just the date part of the **visit_date** column, ignoring the time portion. This groups the visits by day.
- **COUNT(\*)**: This counts the number of visits for each day.
- **GROUP BY visit_day**: This groups the data by the day.
- **ORDER BY visit_day**: This sorts the result set by the date in ascending order.

This query will return a result like this:

MASTERING SQL QUERIES FOR DATA SCIENCE

| visit_day | total_visits |
|-----------|--------------|
| 2023-06-01 | 1234 |
| 2023-06-02 | 1567 |
| 2023-06-03 | 1110 |
| 2023-06-04 | 1348 |

Each row represents the total number of visits to the website for a particular day.

### *Advanced Example: Filtering Visits Based on Criteria*

Suppose you only want to calculate the total visits for days where there were more than 1000 visits. You can use the **HAVING** clause to filter the aggregated results:

sql
Copy
```sql
SELECT DATE(visit_date) AS visit_day, COUNT(*) AS total_visits
FROM WebsiteTraffic
GROUP BY visit_day
HAVING COUNT(*) > 1000
ORDER BY visit_day;
```
This query will return only the days where the number of visits exceeded 1000, filtering out the days with fewer visits.

In this chapter, you learned how to aggregate data using SQL's powerful aggregation functions, including **COUNT, SUM, AVG, MAX**, and **MIN**. You also discovered how to group data using the **GROUP BY** clause and filter aggregated results using the **HAVING** clause. These concepts are fundamental for analyzing large datasets and deriving meaningful insights.

Through the real-world example of website traffic data, you saw how to apply these techniques to calculate the total visits per day. As you continue to explore SQL, these aggregation techniques will become essential tools for summarizing data and performing deeper analysis.

In the next chapter, we will explore more advanced techniques for querying data, including joining multiple tables to extract even more complex insights from your datasets.

# Chapter 5: Joining Tables: Inner and Outer Joins

In this chapter, we'll explore how to work with **multiple tables** in SQL by using **joins**. SQL joins are crucial for combining data from different tables based on a common column. As a data scientist, being able to effectively join tables is one of the key skills you'll need to work with relational databases and extract meaningful insights from complex data relationships.

## Understanding the Concept of Table Relationships

In relational databases, tables are often related to one another. These relationships are crucial for structuring and querying data across multiple tables. The most common types of relationships between tables are:

### 1. One-to-One Relationship

In a **one-to-one** relationship, each row in one table corresponds to exactly one row in another table. This relationship is often used when you need to split data into two tables for efficiency or security reasons.

**Example**: A **Person** table and a **Passport** table, where each person has one unique passport, and each passport is assigned to only one person.

## *2. One-to-Many Relationship*

In a **one-to-many** relationship, one row in a table can be related to multiple rows in another table. This is the most common type of relationship in relational databases.

**Example**: A **Customer** table and an **Orders** table, where one customer can have many orders, but each order can only belong to one customer.

## *3. Many-to-Many Relationship*

In a **many-to-many** relationship, multiple rows in one table can be related to multiple rows in another table. This relationship is typically handled using a **junction table** that breaks the relationship into multiple one-to-many relationships.

**Example**: A **Students** table and a **Courses** table, where each student can enroll in multiple courses, and each course can have multiple students.

# INNER JOIN, LEFT JOIN, RIGHT JOIN, and FULL OUTER JOIN

Joins in SQL allow you to combine data from two or more tables based on a common column. Each type of join returns a different subset of the data. Below are the most commonly used join types:

## 1. INNER JOIN

The **INNER JOIN** returns only the rows that have matching values in both tables. This is the most commonly used type of join.

- **Syntax**:

```sql
Copy
SELECT column1, column2, ...
FROM table1
INNER JOIN table2
ON table1.column = table2.column;
```

- **Example**: Suppose you have a **Customers** table and an **Orders** table, and you want to retrieve data where there is a matching **CustomerID** in both tables:

```sql
Copy
SELECT Customers.customer_name, Orders.order_id, Orders.order_date
FROM Customers
INNER JOIN Orders
ON Customers.customer_id = Orders.customer_id;
```

This query will return only the customers who have placed orders. If a customer hasn't placed any orders, they won't appear in the results.

## 2. LEFT JOIN (or LEFT OUTER JOIN)

The **LEFT JOIN** returns all rows from the left table (the first table in the query), and the matching rows from the right table (the second table). If there is no match, **NULL** values are returned for columns from the right table.

- **Syntax**:

```sql
Copy
SELECT column1, column2, ...
FROM table1
LEFT JOIN table2
ON table1.column = table2.column;
```

- **Example**: If you want to list all customers and their orders, but also include customers who have not placed any orders, you can use a **LEFT JOIN**:

```sql
Copy
SELECT Customers.customer_name, Orders.order_id, Orders.order_date
FROM Customers
LEFT JOIN Orders
ON Customers.customer_id = Orders.customer_id;
```

This query will return all customers, even those who haven't placed any orders. For customers without orders, the **order_id** and **order_date** columns will show **NULL**.

## 3. RIGHT JOIN (or RIGHT OUTER JOIN)

The **RIGHT JOIN** is the opposite of the **LEFT JOIN**. It returns all rows from the right table, and the matching rows from the left table. If there is no match, **NULL** values are returned for columns from the left table.

- **Syntax**:

```
sql
Copy
SELECT column1, column2, ...
FROM table1
RIGHT JOIN table2
ON table1.column = table2.column;
```

- **Example**: If you want to retrieve all orders and the customers who placed them, but also include orders that have not been linked to a customer (in case of data issues), you can use a **RIGHT JOIN**:

```
sql
Copy
SELECT Customers.customer_name, Orders.order_id, Orders.order_date
FROM Customers
RIGHT JOIN Orders
ON Customers.customer_id = Orders.customer_id;
```

This query will return all orders, including those that may not have a corresponding customer. For those rows, the **customer_name** will be **NULL**.

## 4. FULL OUTER JOIN

A **FULL OUTER JOIN** returns all rows from both the left and right tables. Where there is no match, **NULL** values are returned for columns from the table that doesn't have a matching row.

- **Syntax**:

```sql
Copy
SELECT column1, column2, ...
FROM table1
FULL OUTER JOIN table2
ON table1.column = table2.column;
```

- **Example**: To retrieve all customers and all orders, including customers without orders and orders without customers, you can use a **FULL OUTER JOIN**:

```sql
Copy
SELECT Customers.customer_name, Orders.order_id, Orders.order_date
FROM Customers
FULL OUTER JOIN Orders
ON Customers.customer_id = Orders.customer_id;
```

This query will return all customers and all orders. If a customer hasn't placed an order, the **order_id** and **order_date** will be **NULL**. Likewise, if an order doesn't have a corresponding customer, the **customer_name** will be **NULL**.

## Joining Multiple Tables to Combine Data

In many real-world scenarios, you'll need to join more than two tables to combine data. You can chain multiple joins together to retrieve data from three or more tables.

***Example:***

Suppose you have three tables: **Customers**, **Orders**, and **Products**. To retrieve information about customers, their orders, and the products they purchased, you can join all three tables using multiple joins:

```sql
Copy
SELECT Customers.customer_name, Orders.order_id, Products.product_name,
Orders.order_date
FROM Customers
INNER JOIN Orders
ON Customers.customer_id = Orders.customer_id
INNER JOIN Products
ON Orders.product_id = Products.product_id;
```

This query will return a result set that combines data from the three tables, showing customer names, order IDs, product names, and the date of the order.

## Real-World Example: Merging Customer Data with Order History to Analyze Purchasing Behavior

Let's consider a real-world scenario where we have two tables: **Customers** and **Orders**. We want to analyze the purchasing behavior of customers by merging the customer data with their order history.

*Table Structure:*

- **Customers** table:
    - ○ **customer_id**: Unique identifier for each customer.
    - ○ **customer_name**: Name of the customer.
    - ○ **email**: Customer's email address.
- **Orders** table:
    - ○ **order_id**: Unique identifier for each order.
    - ○ **customer_id**: Foreign key referencing **Customers**.
    - ○ **order_date**: Date when the order was placed.
    - ○ **total_amount**: Total value of the order.

*Objective:*

We want to analyze the total spending per customer and the number of orders placed. We'll use an **INNER JOIN** to merge the customer data with their corresponding order history, and then use aggregation to calculate the total spending and order count per customer.

## SQL Query:

sql

Copy

```
SELECT Customers.customer_name, COUNT(Orders.order_id) AS number_of_orders, SUM(Orders.total_amount) AS total_spent
FROM Customers
INNER JOIN Orders
ON Customers.customer_id = Orders.customer_id
GROUP BY Customers.customer_name;
```

## Explanation:

- **INNER JOIN**: Combines the **Customers** and **Orders** tables on the **customer_id** column, returning only the customers who have placed orders.
- **COUNT(Orders.order_id)**: Counts the number of orders placed by each customer.
- **SUM(Orders.total_amount)**: Sums the total amount spent by each customer.
- **GROUP BY**: Groups the data by **customer_name**, ensuring that the total number of orders and the total amount spent are calculated for each individual customer.

## Example Output:

| customer_name | number_of_orders | total_spent |
| --- | --- | --- |
| Alice | 5 | 450.00 |

| customer_name | number_of_orders | total_spent |
|---|---|---|
| Bob | 3 | 300.00 |
| Charlie | 8 | 1200.00 |

This query will return the customer names, the number of orders they've placed, and the total amount they've spent, providing valuable insights into customer purchasing behavior.

---

In this chapter, you learned how to use SQL joins to combine data from multiple tables. We covered the most commonly used types of joins—**INNER JOIN**, **LEFT JOIN**, **RIGHT JOIN**, and **FULL OUTER JOIN**—and explored how to apply them to real-world scenarios. We also looked at how to join multiple tables to extract and analyze data from different sources.

Through the real-world example of merging customer data with order history, you saw how to use SQL joins to analyze purchasing behavior, which is a critical step in data science projects. In the next chapter, we will explore more advanced SQL techniques, such as subqueries and nested queries, which will allow you to perform more complex data manipulations.

# Chapter 6: Advanced Joins and Self Joins

In this chapter, we will explore more advanced concepts of SQL joins, specifically **SELF JOINs** and how to combine multiple types of joins in a single query. We'll also delve into the importance of handling complex data relationships, which is a critical skill for data scientists working with real-world data. To demonstrate these concepts, we'll use real-world examples, including how to structure and query organizational relationships in an employee database.

## Understanding SELF JOIN and Its Use Cases

A **SELF JOIN** is a join that allows a table to join with itself. This type of join is used when you need to relate data within the same table, often for hierarchical or recursive data relationships, such as employee-manager relationships or organizational structures.

When performing a self join, we essentially create two instances of the same table in the SQL query, using aliases to differentiate between them.

### *Syntax:*

```
sql
Copy
SELECT a.column_name, b.column_name
FROM table_name a
JOIN table_name b
ON a.common_column = b.common_column;
```

- **a and b**: These are aliases for the same table, allowing us to refer to it twice within the same query.
- **common_column**: This is the column used to define the relationship between the two instances of the table.

## *Example of a Self Join:*

Let's imagine you have an **Employees** table that stores data about employees, including their **employee_id**, **name**, and **manager_id**. The **manager_id** column refers to the **employee_id** of the employee's manager, creating a hierarchical structure.

| employee_id | name | manager_id |
|---|---|---|
| 1 | Alice | NULL |
| 2 | Bob | 1 |
| 3 | Charlie | 1 |
| 4 | David | 2 |
| 5 | Eva | 3 |

To find each employee's manager's name, you would use a **SELF JOIN** to join the **Employees** table with itself based on the **manager_id** and **employee_id**.

sql
Copy

```
SELECT e1.name AS employee_name, e2.name AS manager_name
FROM Employees e1
LEFT JOIN Employees e2
ON e1.manager_id = e2.employee_id;
```

## *Explanation:*

- **e1 and e2** are aliases for the same **Employees** table.
- We join **e1.manager_id** with **e2.employee_id** to find the manager of each employee.
- The **LEFT JOIN** ensures that even employees with no manager (i.e., top-level employees) are included in the results.

## *Output:*

| employee_name | manager_name |
| --- | --- |
| Alice | NULL |
| Bob | Alice |
| Charlie | Alice |
| David | Bob |
| Eva | Charlie |

This query returns each employee's name and their manager's name, providing a hierarchical view of the organization.

## Combining Multiple JOIN Types in One Query

In some cases, you may need to combine multiple types of joins in a single query. By doing so, you can retrieve data from several related tables and structure the results as needed. You can combine **INNER JOIN, LEFT JOIN, RIGHT JOIN**, and **FULL OUTER JOIN** in various ways to handle different data retrieval needs.

*Example: Combining Different Joins*

Suppose you have three tables: **Employees, Departments**, and **Salaries**.

- **Employees** table: Contains employee information, including **employee_id**, **name**, and **department_id**.
- **Departments** table: Contains **department_id** and **department_name**.
- **Salaries** table: Contains **employee_id** and **salary**.

You want to retrieve the names of employees, their department, and their salary. If some employees are missing salary information, you still want to include them in the results.

You can use a combination of **INNER JOIN** and **LEFT JOIN** to achieve this:

sql

Copy

```
SELECT e.name AS employee_name, d.department_name, s.salary
FROM Employees e
INNER JOIN Departments d ON e.department_id = d.department_id
LEFT JOIN Salaries s ON e.employee_id = s.employee_id;
```

## *Explanation:*

- The **INNER JOIN** between **Employees** and **Departments** ensures that only employees who belong to a department are included.
- The **LEFT JOIN** between **Employees** and **Salaries** ensures that all employees are included, even if they don't have salary data (their salary will show as **NULL**).

## *Output:*

**employee_name department_name salary**

| employee_name | department_name | salary |
|---|---|---|
| Alice | HR | 50000 |
| Bob | IT | 60000 |
| Charlie | IT | NULL |
| David | Sales | 55000 |

In this example:

- Alice, Bob, and David are included with their respective salaries.
- Charlie is included without salary information, demonstrating how the **LEFT JOIN** preserves rows even when there's no matching data in the **Salaries** table.

---

# Handling Complex Data Relationships in Data Science Projects

As data scientists, we frequently encounter complex data relationships that require careful handling through SQL joins. These relationships may involve hierarchical structures, such as employee-manager hierarchies or customer-product interactions, or may require joining multiple tables to combine data from different sources.

Here are a few strategies for managing complex data relationships:

### *1. Handling Hierarchical Data*
Hierarchical data, such as organization structures or product categories, can be represented using self joins or recursive queries (in some databases that support recursive CTEs). A self join helps in situations where a record refers to another record in the same table, like an employee referring to their manager.

### *2. Joining Multiple Tables*

When working with multiple tables, use a combination of **INNER JOIN**, **LEFT JOIN**, and **RIGHT JOIN** depending on the nature of the relationship and the completeness of your data. This allows you to capture the data from related tables while preserving the integrity of your analysis.

### 3. Dealing with Missing Data

Often, data will be missing in one or more of the joined tables. In such cases, using **LEFT JOIN** can help you retain all rows from the main table and include NULLs for missing data. Alternatively, you can filter out rows with NULL values using the **WHERE** clause if missing data is not useful for the analysis.

---

## Real-World Example: Using SELF JOIN to Find the Reporting Structure in an Employee Database

Let's look at a practical example of using a **SELF JOIN** to analyze an employee reporting structure. In a company's **Employees** table, there might be an **employee_id** and a **manager_id**. The **manager_id** refers to another employee's **employee_id**, establishing a hierarchy of employees and their managers.

### Table Structure:

| employee_id | name | manager_id |
|---|---|---|
| 1 | Alice | NULL |
| 2 | Bob | 1 |
| 3 | Charlie | 1 |
| 4 | David | 2 |
| 5 | Eva | 3 |

We want to use a **SELF JOIN** to determine the reporting structure, i.e., who reports to whom in the organization.

### SQL Query:

```sql
Copy
SELECT e1.name AS employee_name, e2.name AS manager_name
FROM Employees e1
LEFT JOIN Employees e2
ON e1.manager_id = e2.employee_id;
```

### Explanation:

- **e1** and **e2** are aliases for the **Employees** table.
- We join **e1.manager_id** with **e2.employee_id** to get the name of the manager for each employee.
- The **LEFT JOIN** ensures that even employees without a manager (like Alice) will be included in the results.

*Output:*

**employee_name manager_name**

| employee_name | manager_name |
|---|---|
| Alice | NULL |
| Bob | Alice |
| Charlie | Alice |
| David | Bob |
| Eva | Charlie |

This query shows the reporting structure where each employee is paired with their respective manager, using the **SELF JOIN** to link the **manager_id** to the **employee_id**.

---

In this chapter, we explored **SELF JOINS** and how they are used to represent hierarchical or recursive relationships within the same table. We also looked at how to combine multiple types of joins (like **INNER JOIN**, **LEFT JOIN**, and **RIGHT JOIN**) to work with complex data relationships. By understanding and applying these join techniques, you can more effectively query and analyze complex datasets, particularly in situations involving hierarchical structures or multiple related tables.

In the next chapter, we will delve deeper into more advanced SQL concepts, such as subqueries and nested queries, which will help you perform even more powerful data manipulations.

# Chapter 7: Subqueries and Nested Queries

Subqueries and nested queries are advanced SQL techniques that allow you to perform more complex data retrieval, filtering, and aggregation. These queries enable you to write SQL commands within other SQL commands, providing a more efficient and flexible way to handle multi-step queries.

In this chapter, we will explore how to write and use subqueries in various parts of SQL statements, their use cases, performance considerations, and a real-world example to showcase their power.

## Writing Subqueries in the SELECT, FROM, WHERE, and HAVING Clauses

A **subquery** is a query embedded inside another SQL query. It is a powerful tool for data analysis because it allows you to perform operations that would otherwise require multiple steps in a single query. Subqueries can be placed in different clauses depending on their purpose, such as **SELECT**, **FROM**, **WHERE**, or **HAVING**.

### 1. Subqueries in the SELECT Clause
You can use a subquery in the **SELECT** clause to calculate or retrieve a derived value that is related to the main query. The

subquery runs for each row of the outer query, and its result is used in the SELECT statement.

Syntax:

sql

Copy

SELECT column1, (SELECT aggregate_function(column2) FROM table2 WHERE condition) AS derived_column
FROM table1;

Example:

Imagine you have two tables: **Orders** (with **order_id**, **customer_id**, and **order_date**) and **Payments** (with **payment_id**, **order_id**, and **payment_amount**). You want to retrieve the **order_id** along with the total payment amount for each order.

sql

Copy

```
SELECT order_id,
    (SELECT SUM(payment_amount)
    FROM Payments
    WHERE Payments.order_id = Orders.order_id) AS total_payment
FROM Orders;
```

This query will return the **order_id** and the total **payment_amount** for each order. The subquery calculates the sum of payments for each order.

## 2. Subqueries in the FROM Clause

Subqueries can also be used in the **FROM** clause. When used in this way, the subquery acts as a virtual table or derived table, which can be joined with other tables in the main query.

**Syntax:**

```
sql
Copy
SELECT column1, column2
FROM (SELECT column1, column2 FROM table1 WHERE condition) AS subquery_alias;
```

**Example:**

Suppose you want to analyze the average **order_amount** from the **Orders** table but want to exclude orders placed by customers from a particular region.

```
sql
Copy
SELECT customer_id, AVG(order_amount)
FROM (SELECT customer_id, order_amount
    FROM Orders
    WHERE region <> 'East') AS filtered_orders
GROUP BY customer_id;
```

Here, the subquery filters out orders from the **East** region, and the main query calculates the average **order_amount** for each customer.

### 3. Subqueries in the WHERE Clause

Subqueries in the **WHERE** clause are typically used to filter results based on conditions that depend on the result of another query.

These subqueries return a single value or a set of values that are compared to the outer query's values.

sql

Copy

```
SELECT column1
FROM table1
WHERE column2 = (SELECT column2 FROM table2 WHERE condition);
```

Example:

Let's say you have a **Customers** table with **customer_id** and **city**, and a **Sales** table with **sale_id**, **customer_id**, and **sale_amount**. You want to find the customers who made purchases exceeding $500.

sql

Copy

```
SELECT customer_id
FROM Customers
WHERE customer_id IN (SELECT customer_id
        FROM Sales
        WHERE sale_amount > 500);
```

This query will return the **customer_id** for customers who made purchases greater than $500 by using a subquery in the **WHERE** clause.

### 4. Subqueries in the HAVING Clause

You can use subqueries in the **HAVING** clause to filter results after the data has been grouped. This is particularly useful when you want to filter aggregated data.

**Syntax:**

sql

Copy

```
SELECT column1, aggregate_function(column2)
FROM table1
GROUP BY column1
HAVING aggregate_function(column2) > (SELECT aggregate_function(column2) FROM table2 WHERE condition);
```

**Example:**

Let's say you want to find customers who have made purchases above the average sale amount. You can use a subquery in the **HAVING** clause to compare each customer's total purchases against the overall average.

sql

Copy

```
SELECT customer_id, SUM(sale_amount) AS total_spent
FROM Sales
GROUP BY customer_id
HAVING SUM(sale_amount) > (SELECT AVG(sale_amount) FROM Sales);
```

This query returns the **customer_id** and **total_spent** for customers who have spent more than the average amount in **Sales**.

## Using Subqueries for Data Filtering and Aggregation

Subqueries are often used for filtering data based on complex conditions or for aggregating data at different levels. Here are a few use cases:

### *1. Filtering Data Using Subqueries*

You can use subqueries in the **WHERE** clause to filter data based on dynamic conditions that depend on data from other tables. For instance, you can filter results by comparing a value against the result of another query.

Example:

To find customers who have placed orders exceeding the average order amount:

```sql
Copy
SELECT customer_id
FROM Orders
WHERE order_amount > (SELECT AVG(order_amount) FROM Orders);
```

This query filters customers who placed orders above the average order amount.

### *2. Aggregating Data Using Subqueries*

You can also use subqueries to perform aggregation operations, such as calculating sums, averages, or counts, on subsets of data, and then use those results in the outer query.

**Example:**

To find customers who have made purchases exceeding the total purchases of a specific customer (e.g., "Alice"):

```sql
Copy
SELECT customer_id
FROM Sales
GROUP BY customer_id
HAVING SUM(sale_amount) > (SELECT SUM(sale_amount)
            FROM Sales
            WHERE customer_id = (SELECT customer_id FROM Customers WHERE customer_name = 'Alice'));
```

This query finds customers whose total purchase amount exceeds Alice's total purchases.

---

## Performance Considerations When Using Subqueries

While subqueries are powerful and flexible, they can sometimes have performance implications, especially when dealing with large datasets. Below are some performance considerations:

### 1. Subqueries vs Joins:

Subqueries can be slower than joins, especially in cases where the subquery needs to be executed multiple times for each row in the outer query. Whenever possible, try to rewrite subqueries as **joins**, as joins are typically more efficient.

## 2. *Subquery in SELECT vs WHERE:*

- **Subqueries in SELECT**: These may result in the subquery being executed for each row in the outer query, potentially leading to performance issues.
- **Subqueries in WHERE**: These are generally more efficient because they are executed once and the results are used to filter the outer query's results.

## 3. *Optimizing Subqueries:*

To improve the performance of subqueries:

- Ensure that the columns involved in the subquery have appropriate **indexes**.
- Limit the number of rows returned by the subquery whenever possible.
- Avoid using subqueries that involve large tables or unnecessary calculations.

---

## Real-World Example: Finding Customers Who Made Purchases Above Average in a Given Month

Let's look at a real-world scenario where we have a **Sales** table with the following columns:

- **customer_id**: Unique identifier for each customer.
- **sale_amount**: Amount of each sale.
- **sale_date**: Date of the sale.

We want to find customers who made purchases greater than the **average sale amount** in a specific month, say **January 2023**.

*Step-by-Step Query:*

1. First, we calculate the **average sale amount** for **January 2023** using a subquery.
2. Then, we filter customers whose **sale_amount** exceeds this average using a **WHERE** clause.

sql
Copy
```
SELECT customer_id, SUM(sale_amount) AS total_spent
FROM Sales
WHERE sale_date BETWEEN '2023-01-01' AND '2023-01-31'
GROUP BY customer_id
HAVING SUM(sale_amount) > (SELECT AVG(sale_amount)
            FROM Sales
            WHERE sale_date BETWEEN '2023-01-01' AND '2023-01-
31');
```

*Explanation:*

- The outer query sums the **sale_amount** for each customer who made purchases in **January 2023**.

- The **HAVING** clause compares each customer's total spending to the average spending for the month (calculated by the subquery).
- The subquery calculates the **average sale amount** in January 2023 for the **Sales** table.

This query will return the **customer_id** and the **total_spent** for customers who spent more than the average during January 2023.

---

In this chapter, we've covered how to use **subqueries** and **nested queries** in SQL, exploring their use in the **SELECT, FROM, WHERE**, and **HAVING** clauses. We also discussed how to use subqueries for data filtering, aggregation, and performance considerations.

We demonstrated how to apply these techniques in real-world scenarios, such as finding customers who made purchases above the average amount in a specific month. Subqueries are a powerful tool for handling complex queries, but it's essential to consider performance implications, especially when working with large datasets. In the next chapter, we will explore more advanced SQL techniques, including **window functions** and their use cases in data analysis.

# Chapter 8: Window Functions for Data Analysis

In this chapter, we'll dive into **window functions**, a powerful feature in SQL that allows you to perform calculations across a set of table rows related to the current row. Unlike aggregation functions (such as SUM or AVG), which reduce the number of rows returned by the query, **window functions** allow you to calculate values over a range of rows while retaining the original dataset.

## Introduction to Window Functions and Their Use in Data Science

Window functions are particularly useful in data analysis and data science because they allow for sophisticated computations that involve looking at a "window" of data around each row. These functions are highly versatile and can be used to calculate moving averages, rank rows, calculate cumulative totals, and more, all without collapsing rows into single summary values.

In data science, window functions are often used when working with time series data, rankings, and other scenarios where you need to look at the data in context, such as calculating moving averages, ranking products, or measuring trends over time.

# Using ROW_NUMBER(), RANK(), DENSE_RANK(), and NTILE()

There are several types of window functions that you can use depending on the type of analysis you want to perform. The most common window functions are ROW_NUMBER(), RANK(), DENSE_RANK(), and NTILE(). Let's explore these functions in more detail.

## *1. ROW_NUMBER()*

The ROW_NUMBER() function assigns a unique sequential number to each row in the result set. It's typically used to assign a row number to each row based on the specified order.

Syntax:

sql

Copy

ROW_NUMBER() OVER (PARTITION BY column ORDER BY column)

- **PARTITION BY**: Divides the data into partitions (optional). It resets the row numbering for each partition.
- **ORDER BY**: Defines the order in which rows are numbered.

Example:

If you want to assign a row number to each transaction ordered by the transaction amount in descending order:

sql

Copy

```
SELECT transaction_id, transaction_amount,
    ROW_NUMBER() OVER (ORDER BY transaction_amount DESC) AS
row_number
FROM Transactions;
```

This query will return a result set with a sequential row number assigned to each transaction, sorted by **transaction_amount**.

## 2. RANK()

The RANK() function is used to assign a rank to each row within a partition of a result set. It assigns the same rank to rows with equal values. However, when there are ties, the next rank will be skipped, leaving a gap in the ranking.

Syntax:

sql

Copy

```
RANK() OVER (PARTITION BY column ORDER BY column)
```

Example:

If you want to rank employees based on their sales performance, with ties being allowed:

sql

Copy

```
SELECT employee_name, total_sales,
    RANK() OVER (ORDER BY total_sales DESC) AS rank
FROM Employees;
```

This query will rank employees based on their **total_sales**, assigning the same rank to employees with the same sales amount, but leaving a gap in the ranks for those with tied sales.

### 3. DENSE_RANK()

The DENSE_RANK() function also assigns ranks to rows but does not leave gaps in the ranking. Unlike RANK(), where tied rows cause a gap in the ranking, DENSE_RANK() continues with the next consecutive rank.

Syntax:

sql

Copy

DENSE_RANK() OVER (PARTITION BY column ORDER BY column)

Example:

If you want to rank employees based on their sales performance, but this time without gaps in the ranks, you would use DENSE_RANK():

sql

Copy

SELECT employee_name, total_sales,

    DENSE_RANK() OVER (ORDER BY total_sales DESC) AS dense_rank

FROM Employees;

This query will assign ranks without gaps, meaning if two employees tie for the highest sales, they both get rank 1, and the next highest gets rank 2.

### 4. NTILE()

The NTILE() function divides the result set into a specified number of buckets or tiles. It assigns each row a number indicating its bucket. This function is useful when you need to divide data into equal-sized groups, such as dividing customers into quartiles based on their spending.

**Syntax:**

sql

Copy

NTILE(number_of_buckets) OVER (PARTITION BY column ORDER BY column)

**Example:**

To divide the employees into 4 quartiles based on their **total_sales**:

sql

Copy

```
SELECT employee_name, total_sales,
    NTILE(4) OVER (ORDER BY total_sales DESC) AS quartile
FROM Employees;
```

This query will divide employees into four equal groups, with each employee assigned to a **quartile** based on their sales.

---

# PARTITION BY and ORDER BY Clauses for Calculating Moving Averages

The **PARTITION BY** and **ORDER BY** clauses are key elements in window functions, as they allow you to control how the data is partitioned and ordered for each window function.

- **PARTITION BY** divides the result set into groups, and the window function is applied to each group separately.
- **ORDER BY** specifies the order in which the window function is calculated for each partition.

## *1. Calculating Moving Averages*

A **moving average** is a common statistical technique used to smooth out data by averaging values over a specific time period. In SQL, you can calculate a moving average using the AVG() function combined with the OVER clause.

Syntax for Moving Average:

```
sql
Copy
SELECT date, value,
    AVG(value) OVER (ORDER BY date ROWS BETWEEN 2 PRECEDING
AND CURRENT ROW) AS moving_average
FROM data_table;
```

- **ROWS BETWEEN 2 PRECEDING AND CURRENT ROW**: This specifies that the moving average should be calculated over the current row and the two preceding rows, making it a 3-period moving average.

**Example:**

Let's say you have a **StockPrices** table with **date** and **price** columns. You want to calculate a 7-day moving average of stock prices:

sql
Copy
```
SELECT date, price,
    AVG(price) OVER (ORDER BY date ROWS BETWEEN 6 PRECEDING
AND CURRENT ROW) AS moving_average
FROM StockPrices;
```

This query will calculate the 7-day moving average of stock prices, including the current row and the 6 preceding rows.

## 2. Moving Average with Partitioning

If you want to calculate a moving average by **stock ticker** (in case you have a table with prices for multiple stocks), you can use the PARTITION BY clause to calculate a moving average for each stock separately.

**Example:**

To calculate the 7-day moving average for each stock ticker, partitioned by **ticker**:

sql
Copy
```
SELECT ticker, date, price,
    AVG(price) OVER (PARTITION BY ticker ORDER BY date ROWS
BETWEEN 6 PRECEDING AND CURRENT ROW) AS moving_average
FROM StockPrices;
```

This query calculates the 7-day moving average for each stock ticker, ensuring that each stock's prices are analyzed separately.

---

## Real-World Example: Analyzing Stock Prices Over Time Using Window Functions to Calculate Moving Averages

Let's use a real-world scenario to demonstrate how window functions can be applied to analyze stock prices over time. Suppose you have a **StockPrices** table with the following columns:

- **ticker**: The stock symbol (e.g., AAPL, MSFT).
- **date**: The date of the stock price.
- **price**: The stock price for that day.

*Objective:*

You want to calculate the 30-day moving average for each stock ticker.

*SQL Query:*

```sql
Copy
SELECT ticker, date, price,
    AVG(price) OVER (PARTITION BY ticker ORDER BY date ROWS BETWEEN 29 PRECEDING AND CURRENT ROW) AS moving_average_30_days
FROM StockPrices;
```

## Explanation:

- **PARTITION BY ticker**: This ensures that the moving average is calculated separately for each stock.
- **ORDER BY date**: This ensures that the moving average is calculated in chronological order.
- **ROWS BETWEEN 29 PRECEDING AND CURRENT ROW**: This specifies that the moving average is calculated over the current row and the 29 preceding rows, giving a 30-day moving average.

## Output:

| ticker | date | price | moving_average_30_days |
|--------|------|-------|------------------------|
| AAPL | 2023-01-01 | 150.00 | 152.30 |
| AAPL | 2023-01-02 | 153.00 | 152.50 |
| AAPL | 2023-01-03 | 154.00 | 153.20 |
| MSFT | 2023-01-01 | 300.00 | 305.40 |
| MSFT | 2023-01-02 | 302.00 | 306.00 |

This query will return the 30-day moving average of stock prices for each stock ticker.

In this chapter, we explored the power of **window functions** in SQL, which allow you to perform sophisticated data analysis without collapsing rows. We covered the most commonly used window functions, including ROW_NUMBER(), RANK(), DENSE_RANK(), and NTILE(). We also discussed how to use the **PARTITION BY** and **ORDER BY** clauses to calculate moving averages and perform other advanced analytics.

By applying these techniques to real-world scenarios, such as calculating moving averages for stock prices, you can gain deeper insights from your data. In the next chapter, we will delve into more advanced SQL concepts, such as **recursive queries** and **common table expressions (CTEs)**, which will further expand your SQL capabilities.

# Chapter 9: Advanced Filtering with SQL

In this chapter, we'll explore advanced filtering techniques in SQL, which enable you to perform more complex queries and extract specific data from your tables. We'll cover the **IN**, **BETWEEN**, **LIKE**, and **IS NULL** operators, along with **regular expressions** for pattern matching. These filtering techniques are powerful tools for narrowing down results and ensuring that your queries return precisely the data you need.

## Using IN, BETWEEN, LIKE, and IS NULL for Complex Filtering

### 1. Using IN for Multiple Values

The **IN** operator allows you to filter data based on a list of values. It's particularly useful when you want to filter a column by multiple possible values, without having to use multiple OR conditions.

Syntax:

sql
Copy
```
SELECT column1, column2
FROM table_name
WHERE column_name IN (value1, value2, value3, ...);
```

Example:

If you want to retrieve customers who live in either **New York**, **Los Angeles**, or **Chicago**, you can use the **IN** operator:

sql
Copy

```
SELECT customer_id, customer_name, city
FROM Customers
WHERE city IN ('New York', 'Los Angeles', 'Chicago');
```

This query will return all customers who live in one of the specified cities.

## 2. Using BETWEEN for Range Filtering

The **BETWEEN** operator is used to filter data within a range, which can include numbers, dates, or text values. It's inclusive, meaning that the values at the boundaries of the range are also considered.

Syntax:

sql
Copy

```
SELECT column1, column2
FROM table_name
WHERE column_name BETWEEN value1 AND value2;
```

Example:

If you want to find orders with a **total_amount** between $100 and $500, you would write:

sql
Copy

```
SELECT order_id, total_amount
FROM Orders
WHERE total_amount BETWEEN 100 AND 500;
```

This query will return all orders where the **total_amount** is between 100 and 500, inclusive.

### 3. Using LIKE for Pattern Matching

The **LIKE** operator is used for pattern matching with string data. You can use wildcards to match patterns in text fields. The most commonly used wildcards are:

- %: Matches zero or more characters.
- _: Matches exactly one character.

Syntax:

```sql
Copy
SELECT column1, column2
FROM table_name
WHERE column_name LIKE pattern;
```

Example:

If you want to find customers whose names start with **"A"**:

```sql
Copy
SELECT customer_id, customer_name
FROM Customers
WHERE customer_name LIKE 'A%';
```

This query will return all customers whose **customer_name** begins with the letter **A**.

To find customers whose names contain **"john"**, regardless of where it appears in the name, you could use:

sql

Copy

SELECT customer_id, customer_name

FROM Customers

WHERE customer_name LIKE '%john%';

This query will return customers whose names contain **"john"** at any position.

### 4. Using IS NULL for Null Value Checking

The **IS NULL** operator is used to filter rows where a column contains a **NULL** value. It's useful when you need to find records that have missing or undefined values.

Syntax:

sql

Copy

SELECT column1, column2

FROM table_name

WHERE column_name IS NULL;

Example:

If you want to find customers who haven't provided an **email** address:

sql

Copy

SELECT customer_id, customer_name

FROM Customers
WHERE email IS NULL;
This query will return all customers whose **email** field is **NULL**.

---

## Regular Expressions in SQL for Pattern Matching

Regular expressions (regex) are used for more advanced pattern matching in SQL. Regular expressions are supported by several RDBMS platforms, including **PostgreSQL**, **MySQL**, and **SQLite**, but the syntax may vary slightly.

### 1. Using REGEXP (or RLIKE in MySQL)

The **REGEXP** operator allows you to perform regex-based pattern matching in SQL. It can be used in the **WHERE** clause to filter data based on complex patterns.

Syntax:

```sql
Copy
SELECT column1, column2
FROM table_name
WHERE column_name REGEXP 'pattern';
```

Example:

If you want to find customers whose **phone_number** follows a specific format (e.g., three digits, a hyphen, and then four digits), you can use a regular expression:

```sql
sql
Copy
SELECT customer_id, phone_number
FROM Customers
WHERE phone_number REGEXP '^[0-9]{3}-[0-9]{4}$';
```

This query will return customers whose phone numbers are in the format **xxx-xxxx**, where **x** is a digit.

## 2. Using Regex for Email Validation

You can also use regular expressions to validate or filter email addresses based on specific patterns. For example, to find customers with email addresses that end in **"gmail.com"**:

```sql
sql
Copy
SELECT customer_id, email
FROM Customers
WHERE email REGEXP '@gmail\.com$';
```

This query filters for email addresses that end with **"@gmail.com"**.

## 3. Regex for Complex Patterns

Regular expressions allow for more complex filtering, such as matching multiple possible patterns. For example, to find phone numbers that either start with **"123"** or **"456"**, you can use:

```sql
sql
Copy
SELECT customer_id, phone_number
FROM Customers
WHERE phone_number REGEXP '^(123|456)';
```

This query will return customers whose **phone_number** starts with either **"123"** or **"456"**.

---

### Real-World Example: Filtering Customer Data to Find Users Who Have Signed Up for a Newsletter Within the Last Month

Let's consider a real-world scenario where you want to filter customer data to find users who have signed up for a **newsletter** in the last month.

Suppose you have a **Customers** table with the following columns:

- **customer_id**: Unique identifier for the customer.
- **sign_up_date**: The date the customer signed up.
- **newsletter_subscribed**: A boolean field indicating whether the customer has subscribed to the newsletter.

We want to find all customers who signed up within the last month and have **subscribed to the newsletter**.

*SQL Query:*

```sql
Copy
SELECT customer_id, customer_name, sign_up_date
FROM Customers
WHERE newsletter_subscribed = 1
```

AND sign_up_date >= CURDATE() - INTERVAL 1 MONTH;

## *Explanation:*

- **newsletter_subscribed = 1**: Filters for customers who have subscribed to the newsletter.
- **sign_up_date >= CURDATE() - INTERVAL 1 MONTH**: Filters for customers who signed up within the last month. CURDATE() returns the current date, and INTERVAL 1 MONTH subtracts one month from it to get the date one month ago.

## *Example Output:*

| customer_id | customer_name | sign_up_date |
|---|---|---|
| 101 | Alice | 2023-09-15 |
| 102 | Bob | 2023-09-18 |
| 103 | Charlie | 2023-09-20 |

This query will return all customers who have subscribed to the newsletter and signed up within the last month.

---

In this chapter, we explored advanced SQL filtering techniques using **IN, BETWEEN, LIKE**, and **IS NULL** operators, along with

**regular expressions** for pattern matching. These powerful filtering methods allow you to retrieve specific subsets of data, making your queries more efficient and targeted.

Through the real-world example of filtering customer data to find those who signed up for a newsletter in the last month, we demonstrated how to apply these techniques in practice. As you continue working with SQL, mastering these advanced filtering techniques will be essential for performing complex data analysis and obtaining meaningful insights.

In the next chapter, we will explore how to **aggregate and summarize data** using SQL, which will allow you to extract key insights and trends from your datasets.

# Chapter 10: Modifying Data: Inserting, Updating, and Deleting

In this chapter, we will explore how to modify data in an SQL database using the **INSERT INTO**, **UPDATE**, and **DELETE** commands. These commands are essential for adding, modifying, and removing data within tables, allowing you to manage your database effectively. We'll also discuss the differences between **DELETE** and **TRUNCATE**, and provide a real-world example to demonstrate the practical use of these commands.

## Inserting New Data into a Table with INSERT INTO

The **INSERT INTO** statement is used to add new rows of data into a table. This operation is crucial when you need to populate a database with new information.

*Syntax:*

sql

Copy

INSERT INTO table_name (column1, column2, ..., columnN)

VALUES (value1, value2, ..., valueN);

- **table_name**: The name of the table where you want to insert data.
- **column1, column2, ..., columnN**: The columns where the corresponding values will be inserted.

- **value1, value2, ..., valueN**: The actual values to insert into the table.

### *Example:*

Let's say you have a **Customers** table with the following columns: **customer_id**, **customer_name**, **email**, and **phone_number**. To insert a new customer's information:

sql

Copy

INSERT INTO Customers (customer_name, email, phone_number)

VALUES ('Alice Johnson', 'alice.johnson@example.com', '123-456-7890');

This query inserts a new customer, **Alice Johnson**, into the **Customers** table. The **customer_id** column will auto-increment (if it's set as an auto-generated primary key), so you don't need to provide a value for it.

### *Inserting Multiple Rows:*

You can also insert multiple rows in a single query:

sql

Copy

INSERT INTO Customers (customer_name, email, phone_number)

VALUES

('Bob Smith', 'bob.smith@example.com', '234-567-8901'),

('Charlie Davis', 'charlie.davis@example.com', '345-678-9012');

This query will insert two new customers into the **Customers** table in one go.

## Updating Existing Data with UPDATE

The **UPDATE** statement is used to modify existing data within a table. You can update one or more columns for one or more rows based on a condition.

*Syntax:*

sql

Copy

UPDATE table_name

SET column1 = value1, column2 = value2, ..., columnN = valueN

WHERE condition;

- **SET**: Specifies the columns to update and their new values.
- **WHERE**: Filters the rows to be updated. If you omit the **WHERE** clause, all rows in the table will be updated.

*Example:*

Suppose you want to update **Bob Smith's** phone number in the **Customers** table:

sql

Copy

UPDATE Customers

SET phone_number = '987-654-3210'

WHERE customer_name = 'Bob Smith';

MASTERING SQL QUERIES FOR DATA SCIENCE

This query will update the phone number of **Bob Smith** to **987-654-3210**.

### *Updating Multiple Columns:*

You can update multiple columns in a single query. For instance, to update both the email and phone number of **Alice Johnson**:

sql

Copy

```
UPDATE Customers
SET email = 'alice.johnson@newdomain.com', phone_number = '111-222-3333'
WHERE customer_name = 'Alice Johnson';
```

This query updates both the **email** and **phone_number** columns for **Alice Johnson**.

### *Important Note on the WHERE Clause:*

Be cautious when using the **UPDATE** statement. Without the **WHERE** clause, **all rows** in the table will be updated:

sql

Copy

```
UPDATE Customers
SET phone_number = '000-000-0000';  -- This would update every customer's
phone number!
```

Always ensure that the **WHERE** clause is used appropriately to avoid unintentional updates.

---

## Deleting Data with DELETE and TRUNCATE

The **DELETE** and **TRUNCATE** commands are used to remove data from a table. However, there are important differences between them.

## 1. DELETE

The **DELETE** statement is used to remove one or more rows from a table based on a specified condition. You can delete specific rows or all rows in the table, depending on the condition provided.

Syntax:

sql

Copy

DELETE FROM table_name
WHERE condition;

- **WHERE**: The condition used to specify which rows to delete. Omitting the **WHERE** clause will delete all rows in the table.

## Example:

If you want to delete **Bob Smith** from the **Customers** table:

sql

Copy

DELETE FROM Customers
WHERE customer_name = 'Bob Smith';

This query deletes the row where **customer_name** is **Bob Smith**.

## 2. TRUNCATE

The **TRUNCATE** statement is used to delete **all rows** in a table. Unlike **DELETE**, **TRUNCATE** does not log individual row deletions, which makes it faster for large tables. However, it cannot be rolled back in some databases, and it does not fire triggers.

Syntax:

sql

Copy

TRUNCATE TABLE table_name;

### *Example:*

If you want to delete all rows from the **Customers** table:

sql

Copy

TRUNCATE TABLE Customers;

This query deletes all rows from the **Customers** table. The table structure and its schema remain intact, but all data is removed.

### *Key Differences between DELETE and TRUNCATE:*

- **DELETE**: Can delete specific rows using a **WHERE** clause, and can be rolled back if inside a transaction.
- **TRUNCATE**: Removes all rows from the table and is generally faster than **DELETE**. It cannot be rolled back in some systems and does not fire triggers.

# Real-World Example: Updating Customer Contact Information in a Database

Let's consider a real-world scenario where you need to update the contact information for a customer in a database. Suppose you have a **Customers** table with columns for **customer_id**, **customer_name**, **email**, and **phone_number**.

## *Scenario:*

A customer, **Alice Johnson**, has recently changed her email address and phone number. You need to update her contact information in the **Customers** table.

## *SQL Query:*

```sql
sql
Copy
UPDATE Customers
SET email = 'alice.johnson@newdomain.com', phone_number = '555-123-4567'
WHERE customer_name = 'Alice Johnson';
```

This query will update the **email** and **phone_number** for **Alice Johnson** in the **Customers** table.

## *Step-by-Step Explanation:*

1. **UPDATE Customers**: Specifies that we are updating the **Customers** table.
2. **SET email, phone_number**: Sets the new values for the **email** and **phone_number** columns.

3. **WHERE customer_name = 'Alice Johnson'**: Ensures that only the record for **Alice Johnson** is updated, rather than every row in the table.

***Important Notes:***

- **Always** use a **WHERE** clause in the **UPDATE** query unless you intend to update every row in the table.
- If you need to delete a customer's contact information entirely, you can use the **DELETE** statement with a specific **WHERE** clause.

sql
Copy
DELETE FROM Customers
WHERE customer_name = 'Alice Johnson';

This query will remove **Alice Johnson** from the database entirely.

---

In this chapter, we learned how to modify data within an SQL database using the **INSERT INTO, UPDATE**, and **DELETE** commands. These commands are essential for managing and maintaining the integrity of your database. We also discussed the differences between **DELETE** and **TRUNCATE**, helping you choose the right tool for different situations.

By applying these commands, you can:

- Add new records with **INSERT INTO**.
- Modify existing data with **UPDATE**.
- Remove data with **DELETE** or **TRUNCATE**.

In the real-world example, we demonstrated how to update customer contact information in a database, showcasing how to use the **UPDATE** statement to modify specific records. Understanding how to modify data is a critical skill for managing databases and ensuring data integrity in your data science projects.

In the next chapter, we will explore **subqueries and nested queries**, which will allow you to perform more complex data filtering and aggregation tasks.

# Chapter 11: Creating and Modifying Tables

In this chapter, we will explore how to create and modify tables in SQL. Understanding how to define and structure your data using tables is a foundational skill in working with databases. We will cover the **CREATE TABLE** statement to define new tables, the **ALTER TABLE** statement to modify existing tables, and how to add constraints such as **primary keys**, **foreign keys**, and **unique constraints** to enforce data integrity.

## Creating Tables Using the CREATE TABLE Statement

The **CREATE TABLE** statement is used to define a new table in a database. You specify the table name, followed by the columns that the table will contain, along with their data types and any constraints that apply to the columns.

### *Syntax:*

```sql
Copy
CREATE TABLE table_name (
    column1 datatype [constraint],
    column2 datatype [constraint],
    ...
);
```

- **table_name**: The name of the table you want to create.
- **column1, column2, ...**: The names of the columns in the table.
- **datatype**: The type of data the column will store (e.g., INT, VARCHAR, DATE).
- **constraint**: Optional constraints on the column (e.g., PRIMARY KEY, NOT NULL).

## *Example:*

Let's say you want to create a **Customers** table with the following columns:

- **customer_id**: A unique identifier for each customer.
- **customer_name**: The name of the customer.
- **email**: The customer's email address.
- **phone_number**: The customer's phone number.

Here's how you can define the table:

sql
Copy
```
CREATE TABLE Customers (
    customer_id INT PRIMARY KEY,
    customer_name VARCHAR(100) NOT NULL,
    email VARCHAR(100),
    phone_number VARCHAR(20)
);
```
This query creates a table called **Customers** with the following specifications:

- **customer_id** is of type **INT** and is the **PRIMARY KEY**, meaning it must be unique for each row.
- **customer_name** is a **VARCHAR(100)** field, meaning it can store up to 100 characters, and it cannot be **NULL**.
- **email** and **phone_number** are optional fields, and their length is limited to 100 and 20 characters, respectively.

## Modifying Tables with ALTER TABLE

The **ALTER TABLE** statement is used to modify an existing table. You can add new columns, remove existing columns, or modify the properties of existing columns.

### 1. Adding Columns

You can use **ALTER TABLE** to add new columns to an existing table.

Syntax:

```sql
Copy
ALTER TABLE table_name
ADD column_name datatype;
```

Example:

If you want to add a **date_of_birth** column to the **Customers** table:

```sql
Copy
ALTER TABLE Customers
```

ADD date_of_birth DATE;

This query adds a new column called **date_of_birth** to the **Customers** table, where the column will store dates.

## 2. Removing Columns

To remove a column from a table, use the **DROP COLUMN** clause with **ALTER TABLE**.

Syntax:

```sql
Copy
ALTER TABLE table_name
DROP COLUMN column_name;
```

Example:

If you want to remove the **phone_number** column from the **Customers** table:

```sql
Copy
ALTER TABLE Customers
DROP COLUMN phone_number;
```

This query removes the **phone_number** column from the **Customers** table.

## 3. Modifying Columns

You can modify the data type or constraints of an existing column using **ALTER TABLE**.

Syntax:

sql

Copy

ALTER TABLE table_name

MODIFY column_name new_datatype;

**Example:**

If you want to change the **email** column to allow longer email addresses (from VARCHAR(100) to VARCHAR(255)):

sql

Copy

ALTER TABLE Customers

MODIFY email VARCHAR(255);

This query modifies the **email** column to allow up to 255 characters instead of the original 100 characters.

# Adding Constraints (Primary Keys, Foreign Keys, Unique Constraints)

SQL constraints are used to ensure data integrity in your tables. You can add constraints to tables using **CREATE TABLE** or **ALTER TABLE** statements.

## 1. Primary Key Constraint

A **PRIMARY KEY** constraint uniquely identifies each row in a table. It automatically ensures that the values in the primary key column(s) are **unique** and **not NULL**.

Syntax:

sql

Copy

```
CREATE TABLE table_name (
    column_name datatype PRIMARY KEY
);
```

Or, to add a primary key to an existing table:

sql

Copy

```
ALTER TABLE table_name
ADD CONSTRAINT constraint_name PRIMARY KEY (column_name);
```

**Example:**

The **customer_id** column in the **Customers** table is a good candidate for the **PRIMARY KEY** constraint. In the **CREATE TABLE** statement above, we've already defined it as the **PRIMARY KEY**. If needed, you can add the primary key constraint later:

sql

Copy

```
ALTER TABLE Customers
ADD CONSTRAINT pk_customer PRIMARY KEY (customer_id);
```

## *2. Foreign Key Constraint*

A **FOREIGN KEY** constraint links one table to another, ensuring that the value in a column of one table matches a value in another table. This helps maintain referential integrity between tables.

**Syntax:**

sql
Copy

```
CREATE TABLE table_name (
    column_name datatype,
    CONSTRAINT fk_name FOREIGN KEY (column_name) REFERENCES
other_table (other_column)
);
```

**Example:**

If you have an **Orders** table with a **customer_id** column that links to the **Customers** table's **customer_id**, you can add a foreign key constraint like this:

sql
Copy

```
CREATE TABLE Orders (
    order_id INT PRIMARY KEY,
    customer_id INT,
    order_date DATE,
    FOREIGN KEY (customer_id) REFERENCES Customers(customer_id)
);
```

This ensures that the **customer_id** in the **Orders** table must match an existing **customer_id** in the **Customers** table.

### 3. Unique Constraint

A **UNIQUE** constraint ensures that all values in a column are different, but unlike a primary key, it allows **NULL** values.

**Syntax:**

sql

Copy

```
CREATE TABLE table_name (
    column_name datatype UNIQUE
);
```

Or, to add a unique constraint to an existing table:

sql

Copy

```
ALTER TABLE table_name
ADD CONSTRAINT constraint_name UNIQUE (column_name);
```

Example:

To ensure that each **email** in the **Customers** table is unique:

sql

Copy

```
ALTER TABLE Customers
ADD CONSTRAINT unique_email UNIQUE (email);
```

This ensures that no two customers can have the same email address.

---

## Real-World Example: Creating a Table for Storing Customer Feedback in a Data Science Project

Let's imagine a scenario where you want to store customer feedback for a data science project. You need to create a **CustomerFeedback** table to store customer responses.

*Table Structure:*

- **feedback_id**: A unique identifier for each piece of feedback.
- **customer_id**: A reference to the **Customers** table.
- **feedback_date**: The date the feedback was provided.
- **rating**: The rating given by the customer.
- **comments**: Optional comments provided by the customer.

### *SQL Query to Create the Table:*

sql

Copy

```sql
CREATE TABLE CustomerFeedback (
    feedback_id INT PRIMARY KEY,
    customer_id INT,
    feedback_date DATE,
    rating INT CHECK (rating >= 1 AND rating <= 5),
    comments TEXT,
    FOREIGN KEY (customer_id) REFERENCES Customers(customer_id)
);
```

### *Explanation:*

- **feedback_id** is an **INT** and is the **PRIMARY KEY**.
- **customer_id** is a **FOREIGN KEY** referencing the **Customers** table.
- **feedback_date** stores the date of the feedback.
- **rating** is an **INT** with a **CHECK** constraint to ensure ratings are between 1 and 5.
- **comments** is a **TEXT** field for storing optional feedback comments.

This table structure ensures that all feedback is linked to a valid customer, and that the **rating** is within an acceptable range.

---

In this chapter, we covered how to create and modify tables in SQL using the **CREATE TABLE** and **ALTER TABLE** statements. We also learned how to add constraints to ensure data integrity, including **primary keys**, **foreign keys**, and **unique constraints**. Understanding how to structure and enforce data integrity within your tables is essential for building reliable and scalable databases.

In the real-world example, we demonstrated how to create a **CustomerFeedback** table for a data science project, illustrating how to define columns, constraints, and relationships between tables. These skills will be invaluable when managing data for any type of analysis or project.

In the next chapter, we will explore **indexes** and how they can improve query performance in large databases.

# Chapter 12: Indexing for Performance Optimization

In this chapter, we'll explore the concept of **indexing** in SQL and how it plays a crucial role in optimizing query performance. Indexes are fundamental tools for enhancing data retrieval speed, especially when working with large datasets. We'll discuss how to create and drop indexes, the differences between **clustered** and **non-clustered indexes**, and provide a real-world example of using indexing to speed up query performance in large transaction tables.

## What Indexes Are and Why They Are Important for Query Performance

An **index** in SQL is a data structure that improves the speed of data retrieval operations on a database table at the cost of additional space and maintenance overhead. Think of an index as a sorted list or lookup table that allows the database engine to quickly locate rows based on the values in specific columns. Without indexes, SQL queries would require a **full table scan**, where the database must examine each row of the table to find the requested data. This can be very slow, especially for large tables.

Indexes are important for the following reasons:

1. **Faster Data Retrieval**: By creating an index on frequently queried columns, the database can locate the relevant rows much faster.

2. **Improved Query Performance**: For large tables, indexes can significantly reduce the time required to perform operations such as **SELECT**, **JOIN**, and **WHERE** clauses.

3. **Efficiency in Sorting and Grouping**: Indexes can also speed up operations that involve sorting or grouping data, such as those with **ORDER BY** or **GROUP BY** clauses.

However, while indexes can improve read query performance, they come with a trade-off. Indexes need to be updated whenever data is inserted, updated, or deleted, which can add some overhead on **write operations**.

## Creating and Dropping Indexes

You can create an index using the **CREATE INDEX** statement, and remove an index using the **DROP INDEX** statement. Let's go through how to create and drop indexes.

### 1. Creating an Index

You can create an index on one or more columns of a table to speed up queries that use those columns.

Syntax:

```sql
Copy
CREATE INDEX index_name
ON table_name (column_name);
```

- **index_name**: The name you give to the index.
- **table_name**: The name of the table you are indexing.
- **column_name**: The name of the column(s) to index.

## Example:

If you frequently query the **Customers** table based on the **email** column, you can create an index on the **email** column:

```sql
Copy
CREATE INDEX idx_email
ON Customers (email);
```

This index will speed up queries that filter, join, or sort by **email**.

## 2. Dropping an Index

If you no longer need an index or if it is negatively affecting performance (e.g., because it is not being used), you can drop it using the **DROP INDEX** statement.

## Syntax:

```sql
Copy
DROP INDEX index_name;
```

- **index_name**: The name of the index you want to remove.

Example:

To remove the index on **email** that we just created:

sql

Copy

DROP INDEX idx_email;

This will remove the **idx_email** index from the **Customers** table.

---

# Understanding the Difference Between Clustered and Non-Clustered Indexes

There are two main types of indexes in SQL: **clustered indexes** and **non-clustered indexes**. Understanding the differences between these two types is essential for optimizing query performance.

## 1. Clustered Index

A **clustered index** determines the physical order of data in a table. When you create a clustered index on a column, the rows in the table are physically sorted based on the values in that column. There can be only one **clustered index** per table because the rows can only be sorted in one way.

Characteristics of Clustered Index:

- The table rows themselves are stored in the order of the indexed column.
- **Primary keys** by default create clustered indexes.
- It is ideal for range queries, as the data is stored in sorted order.

## Example:

When you create a primary key on a table, SQL Server automatically creates a clustered index on the primary key column. If we create a clustered index on **customer_id**, the rows in the table are physically ordered by **customer_id**.

sql
Copy
CREATE CLUSTERED INDEX idx_customer_id
ON Customers (customer_id);

## 2. Non-Clustered Index

A **non-clustered index** creates a separate data structure that references the original table. It does not affect the physical order of the rows in the table but creates a logical order. A table can have multiple non-clustered indexes, allowing you to create indexes on various columns for faster data retrieval.

## Characteristics of Non-Clustered Index:

- The table's data is not physically ordered according to the index.

- You can create multiple non-clustered indexes on different columns.
- Useful for columns that are frequently used in queries but do not require physical ordering.

Example:

If you want to create a non-clustered index on the **email** column in the **Customers** table, the rows will not be physically ordered by **email**, but a separate index will be created to make searches faster.

sql
Copy
CREATE NONCLUSTERED INDEX idx_email
ON Customers (email);

---

## Real-World Example: Indexing Large Transaction Tables to Speed Up Query Performance

Let's consider a real-world scenario where you have a **Transactions** table with millions of rows. The table stores data on customer transactions, and you frequently query it based on **customer_id**, **transaction_date**, and **transaction_amount**. Without indexing, queries that filter on these columns can be very slow.

### *Table Structure:*

- **transaction_id**: Unique identifier for each transaction.

- **customer_id**: Unique identifier for each customer.
- **transaction_date**: The date the transaction took place.
- **transaction_amount**: The amount of the transaction.

## *Objective:*

We want to speed up queries that filter on **customer_id** and **transaction_date** to retrieve recent transactions for a particular customer.

## *Step-by-Step Solution:*

1. **Create Indexes**: First, we create non-clustered indexes on the **customer_id** and **transaction_date** columns to optimize filtering by these fields.

sql
Copy
```
CREATE NONCLUSTERED INDEX idx_customer_id
ON Transactions (customer_id);

CREATE NONCLUSTERED INDEX idx_transaction_date
ON Transactions (transaction_date);
```

2. **Optimizing Queries**: Now, when you run queries that filter by **customer_id** or **transaction_date**, SQL can use these indexes to quickly locate the relevant rows, speeding up the query performance.

For example, to find all transactions by a particular customer in the last 30 days:

sql
Copy

```sql
SELECT transaction_id, transaction_amount, transaction_date
FROM Transactions
WHERE customer_id = 12345
  AND transaction_date >= CURDATE() - INTERVAL 30 DAY;
```

The query will benefit from the indexes on **customer_id** and **transaction_date**, allowing the database engine to efficiently locate the relevant rows and return the results quickly.

***Example Output:***

| transaction_id | transaction_amount | transaction_date |
| --- | --- | --- |
| 101 | 500.00 | 2023-08-01 |
| 102 | 300.00 | 2023-08-05 |
| 103 | 1200.00 | 2023-08-10 |

This query will now execute much faster compared to a full table scan.

In this chapter, we explored the importance of **indexing** for performance optimization in SQL. We learned how to create and drop indexes, and discussed the differences between **clustered** and **non-clustered indexes**. Understanding when and how to use indexes is essential for optimizing query performance, especially in large databases.

In the real-world example, we demonstrated how indexing can speed up queries on a large **Transactions** table, enabling faster data retrieval for frequently queried columns. By creating indexes on **customer_id** and **transaction_date**, we optimized the query performance for finding recent transactions by specific customers.

Indexes are a powerful tool for performance optimization, but they should be used thoughtfully to balance read performance with write overhead. In the next chapter, we will delve into more advanced performance optimization techniques, including **query optimization** and **execution plans**.

# Chapter 13: SQL Transactions and Data Integrity

In this chapter, we will explore **SQL transactions** and how they ensure **data integrity** within a database. A transaction in SQL is a sequence of operations that are executed as a single unit of work. We will also discuss the commands used to manage transactions, such as **COMMIT, ROLLBACK**, and **SAVEPOINT**, and the role of **constraints** and **normalization** in ensuring data consistency. We will conclude with a real-world example that demonstrates how to maintain data integrity when inserting multiple rows into a database.

## Understanding the Concept of Transactions in SQL

A **transaction** is a logical unit of work that contains one or more SQL statements. These statements are executed together, meaning that either all of them succeed, or none of them do. The concept of transactions is fundamental for maintaining data consistency, particularly when multiple operations need to be performed together, such as transferring funds from one account to another.

A transaction has four main properties, often referred to as **ACID properties**:

1. **Atomicity**: Ensures that all operations within a transaction are completed successfully. If any operation fails, the entire transaction is rolled back.

2. **Consistency**: Ensures that the database remains in a valid state before and after the transaction.

3. **Isolation**: Ensures that transactions are executed independently of one another, even if they occur concurrently.

4. **Durability**: Guarantees that once a transaction is committed, its changes are permanent, even in the event of a system failure.

### *Transaction Lifecycle:*

A typical transaction follows this lifecycle:

1. Start the transaction.
2. Execute the necessary SQL operations (e.g., **INSERT**, **UPDATE, DELETE**).
3. **COMMIT** the transaction to make the changes permanent.
4. If there is an error or you want to undo the changes, **ROLLBACK** the transaction.

---

# Using COMMIT, ROLLBACK, and SAVEPOINT to Manage Data Consistency

SQL provides several commands to manage transactions, ensuring that changes are applied consistently or rolled back if necessary. Let's look at the key commands used in transaction management: **COMMIT**, **ROLLBACK**, and **SAVEPOINT**.

## *1. COMMIT*

The **COMMIT** command is used to permanently save the changes made during the transaction. Once a transaction is committed, the changes are visible to other transactions and cannot be undone.

Syntax:

```sql
Copy
COMMIT;
```

Example:

If you perform several operations such as inserting data into a table and updating another, you can commit the transaction to make these changes permanent:

```sql
Copy
BEGIN;

INSERT INTO Accounts (account_id, balance) VALUES (1, 1000);
UPDATE Accounts SET balance = balance - 200 WHERE account_id = 2;

COMMIT;
```

This query will commit the changes to the **Accounts** table, ensuring that the data is persisted.

## 2. ROLLBACK

The **ROLLBACK** command is used to undo the changes made during the transaction. This command is essential for maintaining data integrity if an error occurs, as it ensures that no partial or invalid data is saved.

Syntax:

```
sql
Copy
ROLLBACK;
```

Example:

If there is an error in the middle of a transaction, you can use **ROLLBACK** to undo all changes made in the transaction:

```
sql
Copy
BEGIN;

INSERT INTO Accounts (account_id, balance) VALUES (1, 1000);
UPDATE Accounts SET balance = balance - 200 WHERE account_id = 2;

-- Suppose an error occurs here, and we want to undo all changes.
ROLLBACK;
```

The **ROLLBACK** command ensures that none of the changes made during the transaction are saved.

## 3. SAVEPOINT

The **SAVEPOINT** command allows you to set a point within a transaction to which you can later roll back if needed. This allows for partial rollbacks, meaning you can undo part of the transaction rather than the entire transaction.

Syntax:

sql

Copy

SAVEPOINT savepoint_name;

ROLLBACK TO SAVEPOINT savepoint_name;

Example:

Suppose you are performing multiple operations and want to roll back only the first operation if something goes wrong:

sql

Copy

BEGIN;

INSERT INTO Accounts (account_id, balance) VALUES (1, 1000);

SAVEPOINT first_operation;

UPDATE Accounts SET balance = balance - 200 WHERE account_id = 2;

-- If an error occurs, roll back to the savepoint.

ROLLBACK TO SAVEPOINT first_operation;

COMMIT;

In this example, if the **UPDATE** operation fails, you can roll back to the **SAVEPOINT** and proceed with the rest of the transaction, which prevents the partial data from being saved.

---

# Ensuring Data Integrity with Constraints and Normalization

SQL constraints are rules enforced on data columns to ensure the accuracy and integrity of the data in the database. Constraints help maintain consistency by ensuring that only valid data is entered into the table. There are several types of constraints, including:

## 1. Primary Key Constraint

A **primary key** ensures that each record in a table is unique and that no column in the primary key can have a **NULL** value. It is often used to uniquely identify each row in the table.

Example:
sql
Copy
```
CREATE TABLE Customers (
    customer_id INT PRIMARY KEY,
    customer_name VARCHAR(100)
);
```
This table ensures that each customer has a unique **customer_id**.

## 2. Foreign Key Constraint

A **foreign key** is used to enforce referential integrity between two tables. It ensures that the value in one table matches a valid value in another table.

Example:

sql

Copy

CREATE TABLE Orders (

   order_id INT PRIMARY KEY,

   customer_id INT,

   order_date DATE,

   FOREIGN KEY (customer_id) REFERENCES Customers(customer_id)

);

This ensures that each order references a valid customer in the **Customers** table.

### 3. Unique Constraint

A **unique constraint** ensures that all values in a column are unique. Unlike the **primary key**, it allows for **NULL** values.

Example:

sql

Copy

CREATE TABLE Employees (

   employee_id INT PRIMARY KEY,

   email VARCHAR(100) UNIQUE

);

This ensures that every email in the **Employees** table is unique.

### 4. Not Null Constraint

The **NOT NULL** constraint ensures that a column cannot have a **NULL** value. This is useful for fields that must have a value, such as required fields in a form.

Example:

```sql
Copy
CREATE TABLE Products (
    product_id INT PRIMARY KEY,
    product_name VARCHAR(100) NOT NULL
);
```

This ensures that every product in the **Products** table has a **product_name**.

### *Normalization*

**Normalization** is the process of organizing data in a database to reduce redundancy and dependency. The goal is to ensure that data is stored in the most efficient way, making the database easier to maintain and more efficient in terms of storage and retrieval.

There are several normal forms (NF), with each level of normalization addressing different types of redundancy and inefficiencies:

1. **First Normal Form (1NF)**: Ensures that each column contains atomic values and that each record is unique.

2. **Second Normal Form (2NF)**: Ensures that all non-key columns are fully dependent on the primary key.

3. **Third Normal Form (3NF)**: Ensures that there are no transitive dependencies between non-key columns.

---

## Real-World Example: Ensuring Data Integrity When Inserting Multiple Rows into a Database

Suppose you need to insert multiple customer records into the **Customers** table, but you want to ensure that the data is consistent and that no duplicate customer records are inserted.

### Step 1: Create the Table with Constraints

We will create the **Customers** table, enforcing **primary key** and **unique constraints** to ensure that each customer is unique.

sql
Copy
```
CREATE TABLE Customers (
    customer_id INT PRIMARY KEY,
    customer_name VARCHAR(100) NOT NULL,
    email VARCHAR(100) UNIQUE,
    phone_number VARCHAR(20)
);
```

### Step 2: Insert Data with Transaction Management

You need to insert multiple records, and you want to ensure that all records are inserted successfully, or none of them are inserted if an error occurs.

sql
Copy
```sql
BEGIN;

INSERT INTO Customers (customer_id, customer_name, email, phone_number)
VALUES (1, 'Alice Johnson', 'alice.johnson@example.com', '123-456-7890');

INSERT INTO Customers (customer_id, customer_name, email, phone_number)
VALUES (2, 'Bob Smith', 'bob.smith@example.com', '234-567-8901');

-- If the email already exists or any error occurs, rollback the transaction
COMMIT;
```

This transaction ensures that either all customers are inserted into the **Customers** table, or if any issue arises (e.g., a duplicate email), the transaction is rolled back, maintaining data integrity.

---

In this chapter, we explored **SQL transactions** and how they help maintain **data integrity** by ensuring that a series of operations are executed as a single unit. We covered the essential transaction commands: **COMMIT, ROLLBACK**, and **SAVEPOINT**, which allow you to manage changes and maintain consistency in the database.

We also looked at **constraints** such as **primary keys, foreign keys, unique constraints**, and **NOT NULL constraints**, all of which enforce data integrity at the column and table levels. Finally, we discussed **normalization**, a critical concept for organizing data efficiently.

In the real-world example, we demonstrated how to ensure data integrity while inserting multiple rows into a database, ensuring that invalid or duplicate data does not compromise the database's consistency.

In the next chapter, we will explore **views** and how they can be used to simplify complex queries and provide a layer of abstraction over your database schema.

# Chapter 14: Data Normalization and Denormalization

In this chapter, we will explore the concepts of **normalization** and **denormalization**, two critical techniques in database design that help optimize data storage and query performance. We will begin by understanding what **normalization** is, its importance, and how to organize data into the different **normal forms** (1NF, 2NF, 3NF, etc.). Then, we will dive into **denormalization**, discussing when and why it might be necessary in data science and real-world applications. Lastly, we will walk through a real-world example of designing a **customer data schema** for an **e-commerce website**, considering both normalization and denormalization strategies.

---

## The Concept of Normalization and Its Importance for Database Design

**Normalization** is the process of organizing data in a database to reduce redundancy and dependency. The goal is to structure the data in a way that reduces data duplication, ensures consistency, and allows for easier maintenance. A normalized database makes it more efficient to store, update, and retrieve data.

*Why Normalization is Important:*

1. **Data Integrity**: By reducing redundancy, normalization ensures that data is stored in a way that prevents inconsistent or duplicate data.

2. **Minimized Storage Requirements**: Redundant data is eliminated, resulting in more efficient storage.

3. **Simplified Updates**: With normalized data, updates need to be made in only one place, preventing errors and inconsistencies that may arise from redundant information.

However, normalization can sometimes lead to **performance trade-offs**, particularly with complex queries that require joining multiple tables. That's where **denormalization** may come into play, which we will discuss later.

## The Different Normal Forms (1NF, 2NF, 3NF, etc.)

Normalization is a multi-step process that organizes data into different **normal forms (NF)**. Each level of normalization addresses specific types of redundancy and inefficiency in the database schema. Let's look at the key normal forms:

### 1. First Normal Form (1NF): Ensuring Atomicity

A table is in **First Normal Form (1NF)** if it satisfies the following conditions:

- Each column contains **atomic values** (no sets or lists).
- Each column contains only **one value per record**.
- The order in which data is stored does not matter.

Example:

Consider the following table that lists customer orders:

| order_id | customer_id | products |
|----------|-------------|----------|
| 1 | 101 | Laptop, Mouse |
| 2 | 102 | Keyboard, Mouse |

To bring this table to 1NF, we need to ensure that the **products** column only contains a single value per row:

| order_id | customer_id | product |
|----------|-------------|---------|
| 1 | 101 | Laptop |
| 1 | 101 | Mouse |
| 2 | 102 | Keyboard |
| 2 | 102 | Mouse |

This ensures each column holds atomic values.

## 2. Second Normal Form (2NF): Eliminating Partial Dependency

A table is in **Second Normal Form (2NF)** if:

- It is in **1NF**.
- All non-key columns are **fully dependent** on the primary key (i.e., there are no partial dependencies).

In other words, if the primary key is composed of multiple columns, all non-key columns must depend on the **entire** primary key, not just part of it.

Example:

Consider the following table, which stores orders along with customer information:

**order_id customer_id customer_name product**

| order_id | customer_id | customer_name | product |
|---|---|---|---|
| 1 | 101 | Alice | Laptop |
| 1 | 101 | Alice | Mouse |
| 2 | 102 | Bob | Keyboard |

Here, **customer_name** depends only on **customer_id**, not on the entire primary key (**order_id, customer_id**). To bring this table to **2NF**, we separate the customer information into a separate table:

**Orders Table:**

**order_id customer_id product**

| order_id | customer_id | product |
|---|---|---|
| 1 | 101 | Laptop |
| 1 | 101 | Mouse |
| 2 | 102 | Keyboard |

**Customers Table**:

**customer_id customer_name**

| customer_id | customer_name |
|---|---|
| 101 | Alice |
| 102 | Bob |

Now, the **customer_name** is fully dependent on the **customer_id**, not just part of the primary key.

### 3. Third Normal Form (3NF): Eliminating Transitive Dependency
A table is in **Third Normal Form (3NF)** if:

- It is in **2NF**.
- There are no **transitive dependencies** (i.e., non-key columns should not depend on other non-key columns).

Example:
Consider the following table that stores employee information:

**employee_id department_id department_name**

101          10          HR

102          20          Sales

Here, **department_name** depends on **department_id**, which is not part of the primary key. To bring the table to **3NF**, we create a separate table for department information:

**Employees Table**:

**employee_id department_id**

101          10

102          20

**Departments Table**:

**department_id department_name**

10          HR

20          Sales

This removes the transitive dependency and ensures that non-key columns are directly dependent on the primary key.

## 4. Higher Normal Forms (BCNF, 4NF, 5NF)

While **1NF**, **2NF**, and **3NF** are the most commonly used, there are higher levels of normalization, such as **Boyce-Codd Normal Form (BCNF)**, **Fourth Normal Form (4NF)**, and **Fifth Normal Form (5NF)**, which deal with more complex types of redundancy. For most practical applications, **3NF** is sufficient, but higher normal forms are useful for particularly complex schemas.

---

## When and Why Denormalization Might Be Necessary for Data Science

**Denormalization** is the process of introducing redundancy into a database by combining tables or adding redundant data. While normalization is great for eliminating redundancy, denormalization can sometimes be necessary for optimizing **read performance**, especially in **data warehousing**, **reporting systems**, and **data science applications**. Denormalization can reduce the need for multiple **JOINs**, which can be expensive in terms of query performance.

### When to Denormalize:

1. **Improved Query Performance**: For reporting or analytics workloads, denormalization can help by storing pre-aggregated or pre-joined data, making queries faster.

2. **Reduce Complex Joins**: When complex joins across multiple tables are slowing down queries, denormalization can speed up data retrieval by reducing the need for joins.

3. **Use in Data Warehouses**: In data science and data warehousing, where queries are frequently run on large datasets, denormalization can help improve performance at the cost of extra storage space.

*When NOT to Denormalize:*

- If maintaining **data consistency** is more important than performance, you should avoid denormalization, as it introduces redundancy and makes updates more difficult.

- When the data is **frequently updated**, the overhead of updating redundant data can outweigh the performance benefits.

## Real-World Example: Designing a Customer Data Schema for an E-Commerce Website

Let's consider the design of a **customer data schema** for an e-commerce website. The system needs to store customer information, orders, and product data, with frequent queries on customer activity and order history.

### Step 1: Normalize the Database

Start by normalizing the database to ensure data integrity:

**Customers Table** (1NF, 2NF, and 3NF):

| customer_id | first_name | last_name | email |
| --- | --- | --- | --- |
| 1 | Alice | Johnson | alice@example.com |
| 2 | Bob | Smith | bob@example.com |

**Orders Table**:

| order_id | customer_id | order_date | total_amount |
| --- | --- | --- | --- |
| 1001 | 1 | 2023-07-01 | 250.00 |
| 1002 | 2 | 2023-07-02 | 150.00 |

**Products Table**:

| product_id | product_name | price |
| --- | --- | --- |
| 101 | Laptop | 1000 |
| 102 | Headphones | 50 |

**Order_Items Table** (3NF):

| order_item_id | order_id | product_id | quantity |
|---|---|---|---|
| 1 | 1001 | 101 | 1 |
| 2 | 1001 | 102 | 2 |

### *Step 2: Denormalize for Performance (Optional)*

To improve query performance, you might denormalize the data for specific use cases, such as reporting or generating order history summaries:

**Customer_Order_Summary Table**:

| customer_id | total_orders | total_spent | last_order_date |
|---|---|---|---|
| 1 | 5 | 1250.00 | 2023-07-01 |
| 2 | 3 | 450.00 | 2023-07-02 |

By storing aggregated data such as total orders and total spent for each customer, queries that need this data can be executed more quickly without joining multiple tables.

---

In this chapter, we explored the concepts of **data normalization** and **denormalization** in database design. We covered the different

**normal forms** (1NF, 2NF, 3NF), which ensure that data is stored efficiently, with minimal redundancy. We also discussed **denormalization**, explaining when it might be necessary to improve query performance, especially in data-intensive applications such as data science and reporting systems.

Through the real-world example of designing a **customer data schema** for an e-commerce website, we illustrated how to balance normalization and denormalization to meet the needs of data integrity and performance.

In the next chapter, we will dive deeper into **views** and how they can be used to simplify complex queries and enhance data accessibility.

# Chapter 15: SQL Performance Tuning

In this chapter, we will explore the concept of **SQL performance tuning** and various techniques used to improve query execution time and optimize database performance. As databases grow and queries become more complex, performance optimization becomes crucial. We will cover key methods such as **indexing**, **query rewriting**, and **analyzing execution plans**. We will also explore how to use the **EXPLAIN** command to identify and optimize slow queries. Finally, we'll apply these techniques in a real-world example where we optimize a query to fetch the most popular products from a sales dataset.

---

## Query Optimization Techniques: Indexing, Query Rewriting, and Analyzing Execution Plans

### 1. Indexing

As discussed in previous chapters, **indexes** are essential for improving the speed of data retrieval operations. Indexing helps SQL queries avoid full table scans by creating an efficient lookup structure for the data. Indexes are particularly beneficial for queries that filter, join, or sort data based on indexed columns.

- **Use indexes on columns frequently used in WHERE, JOIN, or ORDER BY clauses**.

- **Limit the number of indexes**: While indexes improve read performance, they come with a trade-off in terms of write performance, as they need to be updated when data is modified.

- **Avoid over-indexing**: Too many indexes can degrade performance, as the database must maintain and update each index with every INSERT, UPDATE, or DELETE operation.

Example:

If you frequently query a **Sales** table based on **product_id** and **sales_date**, creating indexes on these columns can significantly speed up those queries:

sql
Copy

```
CREATE INDEX idx_product_id ON Sales (product_id);
CREATE INDEX idx_sales_date ON Sales (sales_date);
```

## 2. Query Rewriting

Rewriting queries is a fundamental technique for optimizing SQL performance. This involves modifying the SQL query to achieve the same result but in a more efficient manner. Common query rewriting techniques include:

- **Using JOINs instead of subqueries**: Subqueries can sometimes be less efficient than **JOINs**, especially when they need to be executed multiple times.

- **Selecting only necessary columns**: Instead of using SELECT *, explicitly list the columns you need to retrieve. This reduces the amount of data transferred and processed.

- **Using EXISTS instead of IN**: In some cases, **EXISTS** can be more efficient than **IN**, particularly when dealing with subqueries.

Example:

Instead of using a subquery to get the sales data for a particular product:

sql
Copy

```sql
SELECT product_name
FROM Products
WHERE product_id IN (SELECT product_id FROM Sales WHERE sale_amount > 100);
```

You can rewrite the query using a **JOIN**:

sql
Copy

```sql
SELECT DISTINCT p.product_name
FROM Products p
JOIN Sales s ON p.product_id = s.product_id
WHERE s.sale_amount > 100;
```

This version of the query will often perform better, especially on large datasets, because the **JOIN** eliminates the need to execute the subquery for each row.

### 3. Analyzing Execution Plans

An **execution plan** provides valuable insights into how SQL queries are executed by the database engine. It details the operations performed, such as table scans, index usage, joins, and sorting, and helps you identify bottlenecks in query performance.

**Using EXPLAIN:**

The **EXPLAIN** statement allows you to see the execution plan for a query. By analyzing the execution plan, you can determine which operations are taking the most time and look for ways to optimize them.

**Syntax:**

sql

Copy

```
EXPLAIN SELECT * FROM table_name WHERE condition;
```

**Example:**

To analyze a slow query fetching sales data:

sql

Copy

```
EXPLAIN SELECT product_id, SUM(sale_amount)
FROM Sales
WHERE sales_date BETWEEN '2023-01-01' AND '2023-12-31'
GROUP BY product_id;
```

The output will show the execution plan, indicating whether the query uses indexes, whether a **full table scan** occurs, or if there are any joins that could be optimized.

By looking at the execution plan, you might identify that adding an index on **sales_date** or **product_id** could improve the query performance.

---

## Analyzing Slow Queries Using EXPLAIN and Optimizing Them

### *Step 1: Identifying Slow Queries*

First, identify queries that are running slowly, especially when working with large datasets. These are often queries involving:

- **Multiple joins**
- **Aggregation operations** (e.g., GROUP BY, COUNT())
- **Sorting** and **ordering** (e.g., ORDER BY)
- **Large result sets**

For example, a query to retrieve product sales data for the last year might take a long time due to a full table scan:

sql
Copy
```
SELECT product_id, SUM(sale_amount)
FROM Sales
WHERE sales_date BETWEEN '2023-01-01' AND '2023-12-31'
GROUP BY product_id
ORDER BY SUM(sale_amount) DESC;
```

This query could be slow if the **Sales** table contains millions of rows and the columns involved are not indexed.

### Step 2: Using EXPLAIN to Analyze the Query

Using the **EXPLAIN** command, you can inspect the execution plan:

```sql
Copy
EXPLAIN SELECT product_id, SUM(sale_amount)
FROM Sales
WHERE sales_date BETWEEN '2023-01-01' AND '2023-12-31'
GROUP BY product_id
ORDER BY SUM(sale_amount) DESC;
```

The execution plan might reveal that:

- The query performs a **full table scan** on the **Sales** table.
- The **sales_date** column is not indexed, leading to inefficient date filtering.
- The query might be performing a **sort** operation, which can be slow without an index.

### Step 3: Optimizing the Query

To improve performance, we could:

- **Add an index** on the **sales_date** and **product_id** columns to speed up filtering and grouping operations.
- **Avoid sorting if not necessary** or use **indexes** that optimize sorting.

Optimized Query:

```sql
Copy
CREATE INDEX idx_sales_date_product_id ON Sales (sales_date, product_id);

SELECT product_id, SUM(sale_amount)
FROM Sales
WHERE sales_date BETWEEN '2023-01-01' AND '2023-12-31'
GROUP BY product_id
ORDER BY SUM(sale_amount) DESC;
```

By creating a composite index on **sales_date** and **product_id**, the database engine can more efficiently filter and group the data, significantly improving query performance.

### *Step 4: Re-checking the Execution Plan*

After creating the index, re-run the **EXPLAIN** command:

```sql
Copy
EXPLAIN SELECT product_id, SUM(sale_amount)
FROM Sales
WHERE sales_date BETWEEN '2023-01-01' AND '2023-12-31'
GROUP BY product_id
ORDER BY SUM(sale_amount) DESC;
```

The updated execution plan should show that the database is now using the **index** for filtering and grouping, resulting in faster query execution.

## Real-World Example: Optimizing a Query to Fetch the Most Popular Products from a Sales Dataset

Imagine you have a **Sales** dataset for an e-commerce platform, and you need to fetch the most popular products based on total sales volume over the last year. This query can be slow if not optimized, especially if the **Sales** table contains millions of records.

### Step 1: Initial Query

The initial query might look like this:

```sql
Copy
SELECT product_id, SUM(sale_amount) AS total_sales
FROM Sales
WHERE sales_date BETWEEN '2023-01-01' AND '2023-12-31'
GROUP BY product_id
ORDER BY total_sales DESC
LIMIT 10;
```

This query retrieves the **top 10** most popular products based on sales volume in 2023. Without proper indexing, this query might take a long time to execute on large datasets.

### Step 2: Analyze with EXPLAIN

Running the query with **EXPLAIN** can help identify performance bottlenecks:

```sql
Copy
```

EXPLAIN SELECT product_id, SUM(sale_amount) AS total_sales

FROM Sales

WHERE sales_date BETWEEN '2023-01-01' AND '2023-12-31'

GROUP BY product_id

ORDER BY total_sales DESC

LIMIT 10;

The execution plan might show:

- A **full table scan** on the **Sales** table.
- **Grouping** and **ordering** operations that are slow without appropriate indexing.

### *Step 3: Optimization*

To optimize the query, we can:

1. **Create an index** on **sales_date** and **product_id** to speed up filtering and grouping.
2. **Optimize sorting** by using an index that supports the **ORDER BY** clause.

Optimized Query:

sql

Copy

CREATE INDEX idx_sales_date_product_id ON Sales (sales_date, product_id);

SELECT product_id, SUM(sale_amount) AS total_sales

FROM Sales

WHERE sales_date BETWEEN '2023-01-01' AND '2023-12-31'

GROUP BY product_id

ORDER BY total_sales DESC

LIMIT 10;

By creating the **idx_sales_date_product_id** index, the query execution time is reduced as the database engine can now use the index for both filtering by **sales_date** and grouping by **product_id**.

### *Step 4: Re-Analyze with EXPLAIN*

Finally, after creating the index, run the **EXPLAIN** command again to ensure the database is using the index efficiently.

```sql
Copy
EXPLAIN SELECT product_id, SUM(sale_amount) AS total_sales
FROM Sales
WHERE sales_date BETWEEN '2023-01-01' AND '2023-12-31'
GROUP BY product_id
ORDER BY total_sales DESC
LIMIT 10;
```

The execution plan should now show that the query is using the **index**, leading to significantly improved performance.

---

In this chapter, we discussed essential **SQL performance tuning** techniques, including **indexing**, **query rewriting**, and **analyzing execution plans**. These techniques are crucial for improving query performance, particularly with large datasets. By using **EXPLAIN** to analyze slow queries, we can identify bottlenecks and optimize them through the use of indexes, better query structures, and other optimizations.

In the real-world example, we demonstrated how to optimize a query that fetches the most popular products from a sales dataset, improving performance through **indexing** and query optimization.

In the next chapter, we will dive into **advanced SQL functions**, such as **window functions** and **common table expressions (CTEs)**, which can further enhance your ability to perform complex data analysis and queries.

# Chapter 16: SQL for Time Series Data

Time series data is crucial in many business, scientific, and data analysis applications. It involves data points indexed in time order, such as sales data, website traffic, stock prices, or any other dataset that involves tracking metrics over time. This chapter will guide you on how to handle and analyze time-based data in SQL, covering key techniques like using **date and time functions**, grouping and aggregating data, and performing time-based analysis. We will conclude with a real-world example of analyzing weekly sales trends for a product category.

---

## Handling Time-Based Data with SQL

Time-based data typically involves **date** or **timestamp** columns that store time-related information. SQL provides a rich set of functions and tools for working with such data, allowing you to manipulate, filter, and aggregate time-based information efficiently.

When working with time series data in SQL, there are a few important things to consider:

- **Time zone handling**: Be aware of time zone differences when dealing with data that spans multiple regions.

- **Data granularity**: Depending on your analysis, you may need to convert or aggregate data by day, week, month, or year.

SQL provides powerful tools to handle and manipulate time-based data, including:

- **DATE, TIME, DATETIME, TIMESTAMP** data types.
- Date functions such as **DATEADD**, **DATEDIFF**, and **DATE_TRUNC**.

---

## Using Date and Time Functions in SQL

SQL offers several built-in functions that can help manipulate and calculate with time-based data. Let's look at some of the most useful functions:

### 1. DATEADD: Adding or Subtracting Time

The **DATEADD** function allows you to add or subtract a specific interval (e.g., days, months, years) from a date.

Syntax:

```sql
Copy
DATEADD(interval, number, date)
```

- **interval**: The type of time unit to add (e.g., DAY, MONTH, YEAR).
- **number**: The number of units to add (positive number for addition, negative for subtraction).
- **date**: The date to which the interval will be added.

Example:

To find the date that is **10 days** after **today**:

sql

Copy

```
SELECT DATEADD(DAY, 10, CURRENT_DATE) AS future_date;
```

## 2. DATEDIFF: Calculating the Difference Between Dates

The **DATEDIFF** function calculates the difference between two dates and returns the result as an integer (usually in days).

Syntax:

sql

Copy

```
DATEDIFF(date1, date2)
```

- **date1**: The end date.
- **date2**: The start date.

Example:

To find the number of days between **today** and **January 1st, 2023**:

sql

Copy
SELECT DATEDIFF(CURRENT_DATE, '2023-01-01') AS days_difference;

### 3. DATE_TRUNC: Truncating Dates to a Specific Granularity

The **DATE_TRUNC** function truncates a date to a specified level of granularity (e.g., to the beginning of the year, month, or week).

Syntax:

sql

Copy
DATE_TRUNC('unit', date)

- **unit**: The level of truncation (e.g., 'year', 'month', 'week').
- **date**: The date value to truncate.

Example:

To truncate the current date to the **beginning of the month**:

sql

Copy
SELECT DATE_TRUNC('month', CURRENT_DATE) AS start_of_month;

To truncate a date to the **beginning of the week**:

sql

Copy
SELECT DATE_TRUNC('week', '2023-07-12') AS start_of_week;

# Grouping and Aggregating Time Series Data

171

One of the most common operations with time series data is **grouping** and **aggregating** the data by time intervals, such as by **day**, **week**, or **month**. SQL provides various ways to group and summarize time series data efficiently.

## 1. Grouping Data by Time Interval

You can group time series data by **year**, **month**, **week**, or **day** using **DATE_TRUNC** or by extracting specific parts of the date, such as year or month.

### Example: Grouping by Month

Let's say we want to analyze the **monthly sales** for a product category from the **Sales** table. The table contains the following columns:

- **sale_date** (the date of the sale).
- **sale_amount** (the amount of the sale).
- **product_category** (the category of the product).

To group sales by **month** and calculate the total sales per month:

```sql
Copy
SELECT DATE_TRUNC('month', sale_date) AS month, SUM(sale_amount) AS total_sales
FROM Sales
WHERE product_category = 'Electronics'
GROUP BY month
ORDER BY month;
```

This query truncates the **sale_date** to the beginning of each month, groups the data by that month, and then sums the **sale_amount** for each group.

## 2. Grouping Data by Week

If you want to analyze data by **week** rather than by day or month, you can use **DATE_TRUNC('week', date)** or calculate the **week number** using the EXTRACT function.

Example: Grouping by Week

sql

Copy

```sql
SELECT DATE_TRUNC('week', sale_date) AS week_start, SUM(sale_amount)
AS weekly_sales
FROM Sales
WHERE product_category = 'Electronics'
GROUP BY week_start
ORDER BY week_start;
```

This query groups sales data by the **week** and calculates the total sales per week.

## 3. Aggregating Data Over Time Intervals

You can also use other aggregate functions to compute statistics over time, such as **average**, **count**, or **maximum**.

Example: Weekly Average Sales

sql

Copy

```
SELECT DATE_TRUNC('week', sale_date) AS week_start, AVG(sale_amount)
AS weekly_avg_sales
FROM Sales
WHERE product_category = 'Electronics'
GROUP BY week_start
ORDER BY week_start;
```

This query computes the **average sales** for each week.

---

## Real-World Example: Analyzing Weekly Sales Trends for a Product Category

Let's apply what we've learned to a real-world scenario. Suppose we have a **Sales** table containing the following columns:

- **sale_id** (unique identifier for each sale).
- **sale_date** (the date of the sale).
- **product_category** (the category of the product).
- **sale_amount** (the value of the sale).

We want to analyze the weekly sales trends for a particular **product category**, such as **"Electronics"**, over the past 6 months.

### Step 1: Fetching Weekly Sales Data

We can use the **DATE_TRUNC** function to group sales by week and calculate the total sales per week.

sql

Copy

```
SELECT DATE_TRUNC('week', sale_date) AS week_start, SUM(sale_amount)
AS total_sales
FROM Sales
WHERE product_category = 'Electronics'
AND sale_date >= CURRENT_DATE - INTERVAL '6 months'
GROUP BY week_start
ORDER BY week_start;
```

This query does the following:

- **Truncates** the **sale_date** to the start of each week.
- Filters the sales data to include only the past **6 months**.
- **Groups** the data by **week** and calculates the **total_sales** for each week.
- **Orders** the results by **week_start**.

*Step 2: Analyzing Sales Trends*

This query will return a result set showing the total sales for each week:

**week_start total_sales**

2023-01-01 5000.00

2023-01-08 5500.00

2023-01-15 6000.00

**week_start total_sales**

2023-01-22 4500.00

...            ...

By analyzing this data, you can identify trends such as:

- **Sales spikes** or **drops** at specific times of the year.
- The **effectiveness** of marketing campaigns or promotions (if you correlate sales with marketing activities).
- Changes in customer demand within the **Electronics** category.

### Step 3: Visualizing the Data (Optional)

After retrieving the weekly sales data, you can visualize it using data visualization tools such as **Power BI**, **Tableau**, or **Python's Matplotlib** library. This can help you spot trends more easily.

---

In this chapter, we explored how to work with **time series data** in SQL, including handling time-based data using functions like **DATEADD**, **DATEDIFF**, and **DATE_TRUNC**. We discussed how to group and aggregate time series data by various time intervals (e.g., by day, week, or month) and how to apply these techniques to real-world data analysis scenarios.

Through our real-world example of analyzing **weekly sales trends** for an **e-commerce product category**, we demonstrated how SQL can be used to perform time-based aggregations and derive meaningful insights from time series data.

In the next chapter, we will explore **advanced SQL techniques**, such as **window functions** and **common table expressions (CTEs)**, to perform even more complex data analysis and queries.

# Chapter 17: SQL for Geospatial Data Analysis

Geospatial data refers to data that is associated with a specific location on the Earth's surface. It is commonly used in fields such as urban planning, logistics, environmental studies, and e-commerce, where understanding the spatial distribution of data is essential. This chapter will explore how SQL can be used to work with **spatial data**, including using spatial data types (such as points, lines, and polygons), querying and analyzing geospatial data, and performing proximity analysis to gain insights from geographic information. We will conclude with a real-world example of analyzing **customer locations** and performing **proximity analysis** to identify service gaps.

---

## Introduction to Spatial Data Types in SQL

SQL databases that support geospatial data provide special data types to handle geographic and spatial information. These data types allow you to store, query, and analyze data based on its geographic location.

Common spatial data types in SQL include:

1. **Point**: Represents a single location in space using two or three coordinates (e.g., latitude and longitude).

2. **LineString**: Represents a series of connected points (e.g., a road, path, or route).

3. **Polygon**: Represents an enclosed area defined by multiple points (e.g., a region, building footprint, or country).

4. **Geometry**: A general-purpose spatial data type used for both 2D and 3D spatial objects.

5. **Geography**: A specialized data type for handling geospatial data on a curved surface (i.e., Earth), using latitude and longitude coordinates.

For databases that support geospatial data types, such as **PostGIS** (an extension for PostgreSQL), **MySQL**, or **SQL Server**, you can use these spatial types to store and perform spatial operations.

### *1. Point*

A **Point** represents a specific location defined by its **coordinates**. Typically, this is expressed in terms of **latitude** and **longitude**.

Example:

To store a customer's location as a point, you might use the **Point** data type:

```sql
Copy
CREATE TABLE CustomerLocations (
    customer_id INT,
```

```
    customer_name VARCHAR(100),
    location POINT
);
```

Here, the **location** column stores the geographic coordinates of the customer.

## 2. LineString

A **LineString** represents a series of connected points. It is useful for representing paths or routes, such as roads or delivery routes.

Example:

To store a delivery route as a **LineString**:

```sql
Copy
CREATE TABLE DeliveryRoutes (
    route_id INT,
    route_name VARCHAR(100),
    path LINESTRING
);
```

The **path** column contains a series of points that represent the route.

## 3. Polygon

A **Polygon** is a closed shape defined by multiple points. It is often used to represent areas such as land parcels, regions, or boundaries.

Example:

To store a geographic region or a service area as a **Polygon**:

sql

Copy

```
CREATE TABLE ServiceAreas (
    area_id INT,
    area_name VARCHAR(100),
    boundary POLYGON
);
```

The **boundary** column stores the coordinates that form the polygon defining the service area.

## Using SQL to Query and Analyze Geospatial Data

Once you've stored geospatial data in the appropriate spatial data types, SQL provides various functions and operators to query and analyze the data. Common operations include **distance calculations**, **proximity analysis**, **intersection queries**, and **area calculations**.

### *1. Querying Points and Proximity Analysis*

One of the most common operations when working with geospatial data is **proximity analysis**, where you determine the distance between two or more geographic points. SQL databases with spatial extensions provide functions to calculate distances between points, as well as determine if a point is within a specific area.

Example: Finding the Distance Between Two Points

To calculate the distance between two points (e.g., between a customer and a service location):

sql
Copy

```
SELECT customer_id, ST_Distance(location, ST_SetSRID(ST_MakePoint(-73.935242, 40.730610), 4326)) AS distance
FROM CustomerLocations
WHERE ST_DWithin(location, ST_SetSRID(ST_MakePoint(-73.935242, 40.730610), 4326), 5000);
```

In this example:

- **ST_SetSRID** defines the spatial reference system (SRID), in this case, **4326**, which represents **WGS 84** (a global standard for geographic coordinates).

- **ST_MakePoint** creates a point based on longitude and latitude coordinates.

- **ST_Distance** calculates the distance between the customer's location and the given point (service location).

- **ST_DWithin** filters the results to return only customers within a **5,000-meter** radius of the service location.

### 2. Using Polygons to Determine Whether a Point is Inside an Area

You can also perform **geospatial queries** to determine if a point is inside a polygon. This is useful for analyzing whether a customer's location falls within a specific service area.

Example: Checking if a Customer is Inside a Service Area
sql
Copy

```
SELECT customer_id, customer_name
```

FROM CustomerLocations

WHERE ST_Within(location, (SELECT boundary FROM ServiceAreas WHERE area_name = 'Downtown'));

In this query:

- **ST_Within** checks if the **customer's location** (a **Point**) is inside the **boundary** (a **Polygon**) of a service area (e.g., "Downtown").

### 3. Spatial Joins

SQL allows you to perform spatial joins to combine data based on spatial relationships (e.g., finding all customers within a certain radius of a service location or determining which products are within a certain region).

Example: Joining Customer Locations with Service Areas

sql

Copy

```
SELECT c.customer_id, c.customer_name, sa.area_name
FROM CustomerLocations c
JOIN ServiceAreas sa
ON ST_Within(c.location, sa.boundary);
```

This query joins the **CustomerLocations** table with the **ServiceAreas** table to find customers whose locations fall within a particular service area.

## Real-World Example: Analyzing Customer Locations and Performing Proximity Analysis to Identify Service Gaps

Let's consider a real-world scenario where we want to **analyze customer locations** and perform a **proximity analysis** to identify gaps in service coverage. We have two tables:

1. **CustomerLocations**: Stores customer information and their geographic coordinates.
2. **ServiceAreas**: Stores the boundaries of service areas in a city or region.

### *Step 1: Defining the Tables*

We will define two tables to store the customer locations and service areas, using **POINT** and **POLYGON** data types.

sql
Copy

```
CREATE TABLE CustomerLocations (
    customer_id INT PRIMARY KEY,
    customer_name VARCHAR(100),
    location POINT
);

CREATE TABLE ServiceAreas (
    area_id INT PRIMARY KEY,
    area_name VARCHAR(100),
    boundary POLYGON
);
```

## *Step 2: Inserting Sample Data*

Here's how you might insert sample data for customer locations and service areas:

```sql
Copy
-- Inserting service areas
INSERT INTO ServiceAreas (area_id, area_name, boundary)
VALUES
(1, 'Downtown', ST_GeomFromText('POLYGON((-73.9866 40.7484, -73.9860
40.7480, -73.9868 40.7472, -73.9874 40.7476, -73.9866 40.7484))', 4326));


-- Inserting customer locations
INSERT INTO CustomerLocations (customer_id, customer_name, location)
VALUES
(1, 'Alice Johnson', ST_SetSRID(ST_MakePoint(-73.9872, 40.7474), 4326)),
(2, 'Bob Smith', ST_SetSRID(ST_MakePoint(-73.9880, 40.7460), 4326)),
(3, 'Charlie Davis', ST_SetSRID(ST_MakePoint(-73.9845, 40.7465), 4326));
```

## *Step 3: Performing Proximity Analysis*

We now want to find customers who are located within a **500-meter radius** of the **Downtown** service area.

```sql
Copy
SELECT    c.customer_id,    c.customer_name,    ST_Distance(c.location,
sa.boundary) AS distance
FROM CustomerLocations c
JOIN ServiceAreas sa
ON ST_Within(c.location, sa.boundary)
```

```
WHERE sa.area_name = 'Downtown'
AND ST_Distance(c.location, sa.boundary) <= 500;
```

This query finds customers located within **500 meters** of the **Downtown** service area and calculates the **distance** between each customer's location and the service area boundary.

### *Step 4: Identifying Service Gaps*

Next, we want to identify customers who are **outside** the service areas, meaning they are not covered by any service. To do this, we use the **ST_Within** function to filter out customers who are not within the defined service areas.

```sql
Copy
SELECT c.customer_id, c.customer_name
FROM CustomerLocations c
LEFT JOIN ServiceAreas sa
ON ST_Within(c.location, sa.boundary)
WHERE sa.area_name IS NULL;
```

This query finds customers who do not reside within any service area and identifies potential service gaps.

---

In this chapter, we explored how SQL can be used for **geospatial data analysis**, including working with spatial data types (e.g., points, lines, and polygons) and using SQL functions like **ST_Distance**,

**ST_Within**, and **ST_SetSRID**. We also looked at how to **query, analyze**, and **perform proximity analysis** on geospatial data to gain insights.

Through the real-world example of analyzing **customer locations** and performing **proximity analysis** to identify **service gaps**, we demonstrated how geospatial queries can be used to optimize service coverage and improve decision-making.

In the next chapter, we will delve into **SQL for advanced data analysis**, such as using **window functions, common table expressions (CTEs)**, and **recursive queries** to tackle more complex data analysis scenarios.

# Chapter 18: Handling Missing Data with SQL

Missing or **NULL** values in a database are a common challenge that data analysts and developers face. Handling NULL values properly ensures that data analysis and querying do not produce erroneous results or fail altogether. In this chapter, we will explore techniques for handling missing or NULL values in SQL queries, focusing on functions like **COALESCE** and **IFNULL** to replace NULL values with default values. We will also apply these techniques in a real-world scenario of cleaning customer data by replacing missing contact information.

---

## Techniques for Handling Missing or NULL Values in SQL Queries

**NULL** values in SQL represent the absence of data. They can appear for a variety of reasons:

- Missing values in the data source.
- Optional fields that do not always have a value.
- Data errors or incomplete records.

SQL provides several ways to handle these NULL values when querying the database. Some of the most commonly used techniques include:

1. **Using IS NULL and IS NOT NULL:**
   - The IS NULL condition is used to filter records with NULL values.
   - The IS NOT NULL condition is used to filter records that have a non-NULL value.

   **Example:**

   ```sql
   Copy
   SELECT customer_id, customer_name, email
   FROM Customers
   WHERE email IS NULL;
   ```

   This query retrieves all customers who do not have an email address (i.e., where the **email** field is NULL).

2. **Using COALESCE:**
   - The **COALESCE** function is used to replace NULL values with the first non-NULL value in a list of expressions.
   - It can handle multiple columns or expressions and return the first non-NULL value.

   **Syntax:**

sql

Copy

COALESCE(expression1, expression2, ..., expressionN)

If expression1 is NULL, SQL will check expression2, and so on, returning the first non-NULL expression.

**Example**:

sql

Copy

SELECT customer_id, COALESCE(email, 'No Email Provided') AS email

FROM Customers;

This query will return the customer's email if it's available; otherwise, it will return the string **"No Email Provided"**.

3. **Using IFNULL** (in MySQL and SQLite):

   o   The **IFNULL** function is similar to **COALESCE** but is more commonly used in **MySQL** and **SQLite** databases.

   o   It takes two arguments: if the first argument is NULL, it returns the second argument.

**Syntax**:

sql

Copy

IFNULL(expression, replacement_value)

**Example**:

sql

Copy

SELECT customer_id, IFNULL(phone_number, 'No Phone Number')
AS phone_number
FROM Customers;

This query will return the **phone_number** for customers where it exists, and for customers without a phone number (NULL values), it will return **"No Phone Number"**.

4. **Using CASE Expressions**:

  o The **CASE** expression allows you to perform conditional logic in SQL queries.

  o It is particularly useful when you need to replace NULL values with more complex logic or multiple conditions.

**Syntax**:

sql

Copy

```
CASE
    WHEN condition THEN result
    ELSE default_result
END
```

**Example**:

sql

Copy

SELECT customer_id,

```
CASE
    WHEN email IS NULL THEN 'No Email Provided'
    ELSE email
    END AS email
FROM Customers;
```

This query replaces **NULL email** values with **"No Email Provided"** while retaining valid emails.

---

# Real-World Example: Cleaning Customer Data by Replacing Missing Contact Information

In a real-world scenario, we might have a **Customers** table that stores customer information such as **name**, **email**, and **phone_number**. However, some of these fields may contain missing (NULL) values. Let's walk through an example where we clean the customer data by replacing missing contact information with default values.

### Step 1: Inspecting the Data

Let's assume we have the following customer data with some missing information:

| customer_id | customer_name | email | phone_number |
|---|---|---|---|
| 1 | Alice Johnson | alice@example.com | NULL |
| 2 | Bob Smith | NULL | 555-123-4567 |
| 3 | Charlie Davis | NULL | NULL |
| 4 | Dana White | dana@example.com | 555-987-6543 |

In this table:

- **Bob Smith** has a missing **email**.
- **Charlie Davis** has both a missing **email** and **phone_number**.
- **Alice Johnson** has a missing **phone_number**.

We want to clean up this data by replacing the **NULL email** with **"No Email Provided"** and the **NULL phone number** with **"No Phone Number"**.

### *Step 2: Using COALESCE to Replace NULL Values*

We can use **COALESCE** to replace **NULL email** and **NULL phone_number** with default values:

sql

Copy

```
SELECT customer_id,
    customer_name,
    COALESCE(email, 'No Email Provided') AS email,
    COALESCE(phone_number, 'No Phone Number') AS phone_number
FROM Customers;
```

This query will replace any NULL **email** with **"No Email Provided"** and any NULL **phone_number** with **"No Phone Number"**.

### *Resulting Data:*

| customer_id | customer_name | email | phone_number |
|---|---|---|---|
| 1 | Alice Johnson | alice@example.com | No Phone Number |
| 2 | Bob Smith | No Email Provided | 555-123-4567 |
| 3 | Charlie Davis | No Email Provided | No Phone Number |
| 4 | Dana White | dana@example.com | 555-987-6543 |

### *Step 3: Using IFNULL in MySQL or SQLite (Optional)*

In MySQL or SQLite, we could achieve the same result using **IFNULL**:

194

sql

Copy

```
SELECT customer_id,
    customer_name,
    IFNULL(email, 'No Email Provided') AS email,
    IFNULL(phone_number, 'No Phone Number') AS phone_number
FROM Customers;
```

The result would be the same as the one obtained using **COALESCE**.

### *Step 4: Using CASE Expression for More Complex Logic*

If we want more complex handling, such as replacing a **NULL email** with different messages based on specific conditions, we can use the **CASE** expression.

For example, if we want to replace NULL emails with **"No Email Provided"** and phone numbers with **"No Phone Number"**, but also check if the customer has provided either piece of contact information, we can write the following:

sql

Copy

```
SELECT customer_id,
    customer_name,
    CASE
        WHEN email IS NULL THEN 'No Email Provided'
        ELSE email
    END AS email,
    CASE
```

```
      WHEN phone_number IS NULL THEN 'No Phone Number'
      ELSE phone_number
   END AS phone_number
FROM Customers;
```

This provides the same result as before, but using a more explicit conditional structure.

---

In this chapter, we covered how to handle **missing or NULL values** in SQL queries, using techniques such as:

- **IS NULL** and **IS NOT NULL** to filter missing data.
- **COALESCE** and **IFNULL** to replace NULL values with default values.
- **CASE** expressions for more complex conditional logic.

Through the real-world example of cleaning **customer data** by replacing missing **contact information**, we demonstrated how to handle NULL values in a practical scenario. These techniques are essential when preparing data for analysis, reporting, and ensuring data consistency in your database.

In the next chapter, we will explore **SQL for recursive queries**, diving into how you can handle hierarchical data and work with recursive relationships using SQL.

# Chapter 19: Advanced Data Aggregation Techniques

In this chapter, we will explore advanced techniques for **data aggregation** in SQL. Aggregation is essential for summarizing and analyzing large datasets, and advanced methods allow you to group, transform, and present data in various formats that are useful for reporting and analysis. Specifically, we will cover:

- **Using GROUP_CONCAT and STRING_AGG** to combine multiple rows into a single string.
- **Pivoting data** in SQL using conditional aggregation.
- A **real-world example** of aggregating survey responses by grouping data into categories.

---

## Using GROUP_CONCAT and STRING_AGG for Combining Multiple Rows into a Single String

Sometimes, you may want to **concatenate** values from multiple rows into a single string. This can be useful when you need to summarize or present data as a list or comma-separated string. SQL provides functions like **GROUP_CONCAT** (in MySQL) and **STRING_AGG** (in PostgreSQL and SQL Server) to perform this task.

## 1. GROUP_CONCAT (MySQL)

In MySQL, the **GROUP_CONCAT** function is used to concatenate values from multiple rows into a single string, with a specified separator between the values.

**Syntax:**

sql

Copy

GROUP_CONCAT(expression SEPARATOR separator)

- **expression**: The column or value to concatenate.
- **separator**: The separator to use between the concatenated values (optional, defaults to comma).

**Example:**

Let's say you have a **SurveyResponses** table with the following columns:

- **response_id** (unique identifier for the response).
- **survey_id** (the identifier for the survey).
- **response_text** (the text of the response).

To get a list of all responses for each survey as a comma-separated string:

sql

Copy

SELECT survey_id, GROUP_CONCAT(response_text SEPARATOR ', ') AS all_responses

FROM SurveyResponses

GROUP BY survey_id;

This query will return a list of all **response_text** values for each **survey_id** as a single string, separated by commas.

## 2. STRING_AGG (PostgreSQL and SQL Server)

In PostgreSQL and SQL Server, the equivalent function is **STRING_AGG**, which allows you to concatenate values from multiple rows into a single string.

Syntax:

sql

Copy

STRING_AGG(expression, separator)

- **expression**: The column or value to aggregate.
- **separator**: The separator to use between the values.

Example:

To achieve the same result as the previous MySQL example but in PostgreSQL:

sql

Copy

SELECT survey_id, STRING_AGG(response_text, ', ') AS all_responses

FROM SurveyResponses

GROUP BY survey_id;

This query will return the same result—a list of all **response_text** values for each **survey_id**, concatenated into a single string, separated by commas.

---

## Pivoting Data in SQL Using Conditional Aggregation

Pivoting data in SQL refers to the process of transforming rows into columns, which is particularly useful when you want to analyze data in a more compact format. While some databases provide a **PIVOT** operator (e.g., SQL Server), you can also perform pivoting using **conditional aggregation** by applying **CASE** expressions in combination with aggregate functions like **SUM**, **COUNT**, or **AVG**.

### *Pivoting with Conditional Aggregation*

The idea is to use **CASE** expressions to conditionally aggregate data based on a grouping column, and then aggregate the results into separate columns.

Syntax:

```sql
Copy
SELECT
    grouping_column,
    SUM(CASE WHEN condition THEN value ELSE 0 END) AS pivoted_column1,
    SUM(CASE WHEN condition THEN value ELSE 0 END) AS pivoted_column2
```

FROM table_name

GROUP BY grouping_column;

## Example: Pivoting Sales Data by Month

Let's say you have a **Sales** table with the following columns:

- **sale_id** (unique identifier for the sale).
- **product_name** (name of the product sold).
- **sale_amount** (the amount of the sale).
- **sale_date** (date the sale occurred).

To pivot this data by month (e.g., showing total sales for each product by month), you can use **CASE** expressions to group sales by month.

sql

Copy

```sql
SELECT
    product_name,
    SUM(CASE WHEN MONTH(sale_date) = 1 THEN sale_amount ELSE 0 END) AS January_sales,
    SUM(CASE WHEN MONTH(sale_date) = 2 THEN sale_amount ELSE 0 END) AS February_sales,
    SUM(CASE WHEN MONTH(sale_date) = 3 THEN sale_amount ELSE 0 END) AS March_sales
FROM Sales
GROUP BY product_name;
```

This query will return the total sales for each product in the first three months of the year:

| product_name | January_sales | February_sales | March_sales |
|---|---|---|---|
| Product A | 5000 | 6000 | 5500 |
| Product B | 7000 | 6500 | 7100 |

Here, the **sale_amount** is conditionally aggregated by month using **CASE** expressions, and the result is pivoted into separate columns for each month.

---

## Real-World Example: Aggregating Survey Responses by Grouping Data into Categories

Let's consider a real-world scenario where you need to aggregate survey responses by grouping the data into categories. Suppose you have a **SurveyResponses** table with the following columns:

- **response_id** (unique identifier for the response).
- **survey_id** (the identifier for the survey).
- **response_category** (the category of the response, e.g., 'positive', 'negative', 'neutral').
- **response_text** (the text of the response).

You want to aggregate the responses by category and display the total number of responses in each category, along with a comma-separated list of the responses in each category.

## *Step 1: Aggregating Data by Category*

We can use **GROUP_CONCAT** (in MySQL) or **STRING_AGG** (in PostgreSQL) to combine the responses in each category into a single string. Additionally, we can count the number of responses per category.

Example (MySQL):

sql

Copy

```
SELECT survey_id,
    response_category,
    COUNT(response_id) AS total_responses,
    GROUP_CONCAT(response_text SEPARATOR ', ') AS all_responses
FROM SurveyResponses
GROUP BY survey_id, response_category;
```

Example (PostgreSQL):

sql

Copy

```
SELECT survey_id,
    response_category,
    COUNT(response_id) AS total_responses,
    STRING_AGG(response_text, ', ') AS all_responses
FROM SurveyResponses
GROUP BY survey_id, response_category;
```

This query will return the total number of responses in each category, as well as a **comma-separated list** of the response texts:

| survey_id | response_category | total_responses | all_responses |
|---|---|---|---|
| 1 | positive | 10 | "Great product!", "Loved it!", ... |
| 1 | negative | 5 | "Not satisfied", "Poor quality", ... |
| 1 | neutral | 3 | "It's okay", "Nothing special", ... |

## Step 2: Further Aggregation with Conditional Logic

If you want to group responses by multiple categories (e.g., positive and negative feedback) and show them in separate columns, you can use **conditional aggregation**.

Example:
sql
Copy
```
SELECT survey_id,
    SUM(CASE WHEN response_category = 'positive' THEN 1 ELSE 0 END)
AS positive_responses,
    SUM(CASE WHEN response_category = 'negative' THEN 1 ELSE 0 END)
AS negative_responses,
    SUM(CASE WHEN response_category = 'neutral' THEN 1 ELSE 0 END)
AS neutral_responses
FROM SurveyResponses
```

GROUP BY survey_id;

This query will return the total number of responses in each category:

| survey_id | positive_responses | negative_responses | neutral_responses |
|---|---|---|---|
| 1 | 10 | 5 | 3 |
| 2 | 15 | 2 | 5 |

In this chapter, we explored **advanced data aggregation techniques** in SQL, including:

- **Using GROUP_CONCAT** (MySQL) and **STRING_AGG** (PostgreSQL/SQL Server) to combine multiple rows into a single string.
- **Pivoting data** using **conditional aggregation** to transform rows into columns.
- A **real-world example** of aggregating survey responses by grouping them into categories and calculating totals.

These advanced techniques are powerful tools for summarizing, reporting, and analyzing data in more complex ways, and they can be applied to various real-world scenarios like customer feedback analysis, sales trends, and survey aggregation.

In the next chapter, we will delve into **recursive queries** in SQL, which are useful for handling hierarchical data and dealing with recursive relationships in databases.

# Chapter 20: SQL for Data Warehousing

In this chapter, we will explore the concepts and practices behind **data warehousing** and how SQL can be used to manage and manipulate large volumes of data for analysis and reporting. Specifically, we will cover:

- **Data warehousing concepts**, including **star schema** and **snowflake schema** design.
- How to use SQL to perform **Extract, Transform, Load (ETL)** operations.
- A **real-world example** of building a **data warehouse** for sales reporting.

---

## Introduction to Data Warehousing Concepts and Schema Design

A **data warehouse** is a specialized system designed for the storage, processing, and analysis of large volumes of historical data. Unlike transactional databases, which are optimized for day-to-day operations, a data warehouse is optimized for query performance and analysis, often consolidating data from multiple sources.

### 1. Data Warehouse Architecture

A typical **data warehouse architecture** involves multiple layers, including:

- **Data Sources**: Various operational databases or external data feeds.
- **ETL Layer**: Extracts data from source systems, transforms it to match the warehouse schema, and loads it into the warehouse.
- **Data Warehouse**: A central repository for cleansed, historical data.
- **Reporting and Analytics**: Tools that allow analysts to query the data warehouse and generate insights.

## *2. Schema Design*

Schema design in a data warehouse is critical for efficient querying and reporting. There are two primary schema designs used in data warehousing: the **star schema** and the **snowflake schema**.

### Star Schema

In the **star schema**, there is a central fact table that stores quantitative data (such as sales or transactions), surrounded by several **dimension tables** that describe attributes related to the facts (such as customers, time, or products). The schema is called "star" because the diagram resembles a star, with the fact table in the center and dimension tables around it.

- **Fact Table**: Stores the measures (numerical data) of business processes, such as sales, revenue, or units sold.
- **Dimension Tables**: Contain descriptive data related to the facts, such as product names, customer information, or time periods.

## Example of Star Schema:

| **Fact Table**: Sales |------------|-----------------|----------------|----------
--| | sales_id | product_id | customer_id | sale_date | amount |

| **Dimension Table**: Products |------------|-----------------|-------------
--| | product_id | product_name | category | price |

| **Dimension Table**: Customers |------------|-----------------|------------
----| | customer_id| customer_name | address |

| **Dimension Table**: Time |------------|-----------------| | time_id | day | month | year |

## Snowflake Schema

The **snowflake schema** is a more normalized version of the star schema. It involves breaking down dimension tables into multiple related tables to reduce redundancy. This structure resembles a snowflake, with the fact table in the center and multiple layers of dimension tables branching off.

While the snowflake schema reduces redundancy and saves storage space, it can make querying more complex because of the need for more joins.

**Example of Snowflake Schema:**

| **Fact Table**: Sales |------------|------------------|----------------|------------| | sales_id | product_id | customer_id | sale_date | amount |

| **Dimension Table**: Products |------------|------------------| | product_id | product_name | category_id |

| **Dimension Table**: Categories |------------|------------------| | category_id| category_name |

| **Dimension Table**: Customers |------------|------------------| | customer_id| customer_name | address_id |

| **Dimension Table**: Addresses |------------|------------------| | address_id | address |

| **Dimension Table**: Time |------------|------------------| | time_id | day | month_id | year_id |

### 3. Choosing Between Star and Snowflake Schema

- **Star Schema** is typically faster for queries, as it involves fewer joins and is easier to understand.

- **Snowflake Schema** reduces redundancy, but it may require more complex queries with more joins and slightly slower performance.

In practice, the star schema is more commonly used in reporting and analytics for its simplicity and speed, whereas the snowflake schema might be used in cases where storage efficiency and reducing data redundancy are more important.

## Using SQL to Perform Extract, Transform, Load (ETL) Operations

ETL stands for **Extract**, **Transform**, and **Load**, and it refers to the process of moving data from various sources into a data warehouse.

1. **Extract**: Data is pulled from different source systems, such as transactional databases, external APIs, or flat files (CSV, Excel).

2. **Transform**: The extracted data is cleaned, normalized, and formatted to fit the structure of the data warehouse schema. This may involve removing duplicates, handling NULL values, or aggregating data.

3. **Load**: The transformed data is loaded into the data warehouse tables, either incrementally or in bulk.

SQL plays a key role in the **Transform** and **Load** stages of ETL, especially when using SQL scripts, stored procedures, or ETL tools (like Apache NiFi, Talend, or Informatica).

### 1. Extracting Data

Typically, extraction involves running queries on source systems to retrieve the necessary data. This can be done using **SELECT** statements in SQL.

sql
Copy
```sql
SELECT customer_id, customer_name, purchase_amount, purchase_date
FROM SalesDB.transactions
WHERE purchase_date >= '2023-01-01';
```

This query extracts transaction data from a **SalesDB** database, pulling information for transactions that occurred after January 1st, 2023.

### 2. Transforming Data

Data transformation may involve operations like cleaning, filtering, and aggregating data. You can use SQL functions such as **CASE**, **COALESCE**, and **JOIN** to transform the data into the desired format.

Example: Cleaning Data (Replacing NULL values)

sql
Copy
```sql
SELECT
  customer_id,
```

```
COALESCE(customer_name, 'Unknown') AS customer_name,
COALESCE(purchase_amount, 0) AS purchase_amount,
purchase_date
FROM temp_transactions;
```

This query replaces **NULL** values in the **customer_name** and **purchase_amount** columns with default values ("Unknown" and 0, respectively).

### 3. Loading Data

Once the data is cleaned and transformed, it is loaded into the target data warehouse tables. This is often done using **INSERT** statements.

```sql
Copy
INSERT INTO DataWarehouse.sales_fact (customer_id, product_id, sale_date,
sale_amount)
SELECT customer_id, product_id, purchase_date, purchase_amount
FROM temp_transactions;
```

This query loads the transformed transaction data from a temporary table (**temp_transactions**) into the **sales_fact** table in the data warehouse.

# Real-World Example: Building a Data Warehouse for Sales Reporting

Let's walk through a real-world example where we build a data warehouse to store and report on **sales data**.

## Step 1: Define the Data Warehouse Schema

Our data warehouse schema will include the following tables:

- **sales_fact**: The fact table, containing sales data (sales_id, product_id, customer_id, sale_amount, sale_date).
- **products_dim**: A dimension table describing product details (product_id, product_name, category).
- **customers_dim**: A dimension table describing customer information (customer_id, customer_name, region).
- **time_dim**: A dimension table describing time (time_id, year, month, day).

## Step 2: Extract Data from Source Systems

We extract sales data from the **SalesDB** transactional database and product data from the **ProductsDB** database.

sql
Copy

```
-- Extracting sales data
SELECT customer_id, product_id, purchase_date, purchase_amount
FROM SalesDB.transactions
WHERE purchase_date >= '2023-01-01';

-- Extracting product data
SELECT product_id, product_name, category
FROM ProductsDB.products;
```

## Step 3: Transform the Data

Transform the data by cleaning it (handling NULL values) and formatting it into the appropriate structure for the data warehouse.

sql

Copy

```sql
-- Cleaning and transforming sales data
SELECT
    customer_id,
    product_id,
    COALESCE(purchase_amount, 0) AS purchase_amount,
    purchase_date
FROM temp_transactions;


-- Transforming product data (e.g., standardizing category names)
SELECT
    product_id,
    product_name,
    CASE
        WHEN category = 'Tech' THEN 'Technology'
        ELSE 'Other'
    END AS category
FROM temp_products;
```

## *Step 4: Load Data into the Data Warehouse*

Finally, the transformed data is loaded into the respective tables in the data warehouse.

sql

Copy

```sql
-- Loading sales data into the sales_fact table
```

```
INSERT INTO DataWarehouse.sales_fact (customer_id, product_id, sale_date,
sale_amount)
SELECT customer_id, product_id, purchase_date, purchase_amount
FROM temp_sales;

-- Loading product data into the products_dim table
INSERT INTO DataWarehouse.products_dim (product_id, product_name,
category)
SELECT product_id, product_name, category
FROM temp_products;
```

---

In this chapter, we explored the key concepts and techniques involved in **data warehousing** using SQL. We covered:

- **Star and snowflake schema** design for organizing data efficiently in a data warehouse.
- **ETL (Extract, Transform, Load)** operations in SQL for extracting data from source systems, transforming it into the appropriate format, and loading it into the data warehouse.
- A **real-world example** of building a data warehouse for **sales reporting**, including the extraction of data, transformation of the data, and loading the data into a structured schema for reporting and analysis.

These techniques are foundational for creating efficient and scalable data warehouses that support business intelligence and reporting applications.

In the next chapter, we will dive into **SQL for Data Governance**, focusing on how to maintain data quality, security, and compliance within your databases.

# Chapter 21: SQL for Data Science Projects

In this chapter, we will explore how **SQL** integrates into **data science workflows**, specifically focusing on how SQL can be used for **data manipulation** and **analysis**. We will examine how SQL can be combined with popular data science programming languages, such as **Python** and **R**, to handle data extraction, transformation, and preparation for more complex analyses, including **machine learning**. To make these concepts practical, we'll go through a **real-world example** of using SQL to query a database and prepare data for machine learning models.

---

## Integrating SQL with Data Science Workflows

SQL is a powerful language for working with relational databases, and it is commonly used in **data science projects** to:

- **Extract** large datasets from relational databases for analysis.
- **Clean** and **transform** the data into a format suitable for analysis.
- Perform **aggregations**, **groupings**, and **joins** for data preprocessing.

While SQL is essential for data manipulation within databases, data science workflows often involve multiple steps, including statistical analysis, predictive modeling, and data visualization. SQL fits naturally into this workflow, especially during the data preparation and exploration phases.

*Data Science Workflow Overview:*

1. **Data Extraction**: Using SQL to query and pull data from a database.
2. **Data Cleaning**: Using SQL to filter, aggregate, and handle missing or inconsistent data.
3. **Data Transformation**: Preprocessing data using SQL functions to convert it into a usable format for analysis or modeling.
4. **Analysis**: Using tools like Python and R to perform statistical analysis or build machine learning models.
5. **Visualization**: Using Python (Matplotlib, Seaborn) or R (ggplot2) to visualize insights.

SQL is an indispensable tool for extracting and transforming data, but once the data is in the right format, Python and R are typically used for more complex analysis, statistical modeling, and machine learning tasks.

# Using SQL with Python and R for Data Manipulation and Analysis

**Python** and **R** are both widely used in data science for statistical analysis, machine learning, and data visualization. Both languages can seamlessly integrate with SQL to manage and manipulate data from relational databases. Below, we explore how to use SQL with **Python** (via libraries like **pandas** and **SQLAlchemy**) and **R** (via packages like **DBI** and **dplyr**) for data manipulation.

## *Using SQL with Python for Data Manipulation and Analysis*

**Python** is an excellent tool for integrating SQL into a data science project, particularly using the **pandas** library. The **pandas** library allows data scientists to perform SQL-like operations on data, but it works in-memory with dataframes. However, you can easily integrate SQL with Python to extract data from a database and then use pandas for analysis.

### Using SQLAlchemy and pandas:

1. **SQLAlchemy** is a library that provides a set of tools to connect to relational databases.
2. **pandas** integrates well with SQLAlchemy to run SQL queries and load the result directly into a pandas dataframe.

### Example: Querying Data with Python

python

Copy

```python
import pandas as pd
from sqlalchemy import create_engine

# Establish connection to the database (replace with your database connection details)
engine = create_engine('postgresql://username:password@localhost:5432/mydatabase')

# Query the database
query = """
SELECT customer_id, SUM(amount) AS total_sales
FROM sales
WHERE sale_date >= '2023-01-01'
GROUP BY customer_id
"""

# Load the result of the query into a pandas dataframe
df = pd.read_sql(query, engine)

# Display the first few rows of the dataframe
print(df.head())
```

In this example:

- **SQLAlchemy** is used to create a connection to a PostgreSQL database.
- **pandas'** read_sql function executes the SQL query and stores the result in a pandas dataframe.

- You can then proceed to clean, transform, or analyze the data using pandas functions.

## Using SQL with Python for Machine Learning:

After extracting the data, you can use it in machine learning models. For instance, after querying the sales data, you might prepare it for training a machine learning model to predict customer churn based on total sales and customer demographics.

```python
Copy
from sklearn.model_selection import train_test_split
from sklearn.ensemble import RandomForestClassifier

# Assume we have already loaded the customer data into a dataframe `df`
X = df[['total_sales']]  # Features
y = df['churn']  # Target variable

# Split the data into training and testing sets
X_train, X_test, y_train, y_test = train_test_split(X, y, test_size=0.3, random_state=42)

# Train a Random Forest model
model = RandomForestClassifier()
model.fit(X_train, y_train)

# Evaluate the model
print(f'Model Accuracy: {model.score(X_test, y_test)}')
```

### *Using SQL with R for Data Manipulation and Analysis*

**R** is another popular tool for data science that integrates well with SQL. The **DBI** package allows R to connect to relational databases and execute SQL queries directly. Additionally, R's **dplyr** package provides a SQL-like syntax for manipulating data within R.

Example: Querying Data with R

```r
Copy
library(DBI)
library(RPostgres)

# Connect to the database
con <- dbConnect(RPostgres::Postgres(), "dbname=mydatabase user=username password=password")

# Query the database
query <- "
SELECT customer_id, SUM(amount) AS total_sales
FROM sales
WHERE sale_date >= '2023-01-01'
GROUP BY customer_id
"

# Fetch the query results into an R dataframe
df <- dbGetQuery(con, query)

# View the first few rows
head(df)

# Disconnect from the database
```

dbDisconnect(con)

In this example:

- **DBI** and **RPostgres** are used to connect to a PostgreSQL database.
- The query result is fetched into an R dataframe using **dbGetQuery**.
- Once in the dataframe, you can use **dplyr** for further data manipulation or analysis.

## Using SQL with R for Machine Learning:

After fetching and transforming the data, you can build machine learning models in R using libraries like **caret** or **randomForest**.

```r
Copy
library(randomForest)

# Assume df contains total_sales and churn columns
X <- df$total_sales
y <- df$churn

# Train a random forest model
model <- randomForest(X, as.factor(y))

# Evaluate the model
print(model)
```

# Real-World Example: Querying a Database to Prepare Data for Machine Learning Models

Let's put it all together with a real-world example where we use SQL to query a database and prepare data for a machine learning model. In this case, we will use **customer purchase data** to predict **customer churn** based on the amount spent in the last 6 months.

### *Step 1: Querying the Data*

We'll use SQL to extract customer data, including **total_sales** in the past 6 months, and whether the customer has churned.

sql

Copy

```sql
SELECT customer_id,
    SUM(sale_amount) AS total_sales_last_6_months,
    MAX(CASE WHEN last_purchase_date < CURRENT_DATE -
INTERVAL '6 months' THEN 1 ELSE 0 END) AS churn
FROM sales
GROUP BY customer_id;
```

This query extracts:

- The **total_sales_last_6_months** for each customer.
- A **churn** flag, which is 1 if the last purchase was more than 6 months ago, indicating the customer has churned, and 0 otherwise.

### *Step 2: Loading Data into Python*

We can use the **SQLAlchemy** library in Python to execute this query and load the data into a pandas dataframe for further analysis.

```python
Copy
import pandas as pd
from sqlalchemy import create_engine

# Establish a connection to the database
engine = create_engine('postgresql://username:password@localhost:5432/mydatabase')

# Query the database and load the data into a pandas dataframe
query = """
SELECT customer_id,
    SUM(sale_amount) AS total_sales_last_6_months,
    MAX(CASE WHEN last_purchase_date < CURRENT_DATE - INTERVAL '6 months' THEN 1 ELSE 0 END) AS churn
FROM sales
GROUP BY customer_id;
"""

df = pd.read_sql(query, engine)

# Display the first few rows
print(df.head())
```

### Step 3: Preprocessing the Data for Machine Learning

Next, we preprocess the data by splitting it into features (e.g., **total_sales_last_6_months**) and the target variable (**churn**), and then train a machine learning model.

python
Copy

```python
from sklearn.model_selection import train_test_split
from sklearn.ensemble import RandomForestClassifier

# Features and target variable
X = df[['total_sales_last_6_months']]
y = df['churn']

# Split the data into training and testing sets
X_train, X_test, y_train, y_test = train_test_split(X, y, test_size=0.3, random_state=42)

# Train a Random Forest classifier
model = RandomForestClassifier()
model.fit(X_train, y_train)

# Evaluate the model
print(f'Model Accuracy: {model.score(X_test, y_test)}')
```

### *Step 4: Model Evaluation*

The output will give you the model's accuracy, which shows how well the model can predict customer churn based on the total sales data.

In this chapter, we explored how **SQL** integrates into **data science workflows**, particularly for **data manipulation** and **analysis**. We discussed how SQL can be combined with **Python** and **R** to query, clean, transform, and prepare data for **machine learning models**. Through a **real-world example**, we demonstrated how to query a database, clean and prepare the data, and build a machine learning model to predict customer churn.

SQL plays a crucial role in data extraction and preparation, and when integrated with Python or R, it becomes a powerful tool in the data science toolbox. In the next chapter, we will explore **SQL for time series forecasting**, where we'll look at techniques for working with time-based data and building predictive models using SQL.

# Chapter 22: Integrating SQL with Machine Learning Workflows

In this chapter, we will explore how to **integrate SQL** into **machine learning workflows**, focusing on how to use SQL for **data preparation**, **extracting training data**, and building datasets that are ready for machine learning models. SQL is a vital tool for querying databases and transforming data before it is fed into machine learning algorithms. We will walk through practical techniques for using SQL to efficiently prepare and extract the right features, and we will conclude with a real-world example of preparing **customer behavior data** for a marketing campaign machine learning model.

---

## Using SQL to Prepare Datasets for Machine Learning

The first step in any **machine learning workflow** is to ensure that the data is properly **prepared**. SQL is a powerful tool for cleaning, filtering, and transforming raw data into a structured format that is suitable for machine learning models. Here are the key steps in preparing data using SQL:

### *1. Data Extraction*

SQL is often used to extract data from **relational databases** and bring it into a more analysis-friendly environment (such as **Python** or **R**). Complex SQL queries are commonly written to pull the relevant columns, filter out unnecessary records, and join multiple tables to form a cohesive dataset.

Example:

To build a dataset for training a machine learning model, you may need data from multiple tables. For example, to prepare data on **customer behavior**, you might need to combine sales data, customer information, and interaction logs. A complex SQL query could join multiple tables and calculate aggregated metrics like total sales or frequency of customer visits.

```sql
Copy
SELECT c.customer_id,
    c.customer_name,
    SUM(s.amount) AS total_spent,
    COUNT(o.order_id) AS total_orders,
    AVG(s.amount) AS avg_purchase_value,
    MAX(o.order_date) AS last_order_date
FROM customers c
JOIN sales s ON c.customer_id = s.customer_id
JOIN orders o ON c.customer_id = o.customer_id
WHERE o.order_date >= '2023-01-01'
GROUP BY c.customer_id;
```

This query:

- Joins the **customers**, **sales**, and **orders** tables.
- Aggregates data to calculate the total money spent, the number of orders, and the average purchase value for each customer.
- Filters the data to include only orders placed after January 1st, 2023.

## 2. Data Cleaning

Machine learning models require **clean data**. You will often need to perform tasks like:

- **Handling NULL values**: Use SQL functions such as **COALESCE** or **IFNULL** to replace NULL values with appropriate defaults.
- **Removing duplicates**: Use **DISTINCT** or **ROW_NUMBER()** to ensure there are no redundant records.
- **Filtering outliers**: Use SQL filters to remove extreme values that may distort your model.

Example:

If a dataset contains **NULL values** in the **customer_age** column, you might replace these with a default value like the **median age** of the customers.

sql
Copy
SELECT customer_id,

COALESCE(customer_age, (SELECT AVG(customer_age) FROM customers)) AS customer_age
FROM customers;

This query replaces **NULL** values in **customer_age** with the **average** customer age from the table.

## 3. Feature Engineering

**Feature engineering** is the process of creating new features (or columns) that will be useful for the machine learning model. This could involve:

- **Creating time-based features**: Extracting **day**, **month**, or **year** from timestamps.
- **Aggregating data**: Creating **grouped** features like **average purchase value**, **total purchases**, etc.
- **Encoding categorical variables**: Converting categorical columns (like **customer segment**) into numerical values.

Example:

To create features related to the **customer's recency** of purchases, we can compute the number of days since their **last order**:

```sql
Copy
SELECT customer_id,
    DATEDIFF(CURRENT_DATE, MAX(order_date)) AS
days_since_last_purchase
FROM orders
```

GROUP BY customer_id;

This query calculates the number of days since the **last purchase** for each customer, which could be a useful feature for modeling customer **churn** or **retention**.

---

# Extracting Training Data Using Complex SQL Queries

In machine learning, preparing the **training data** is crucial. SQL allows you to run complex queries that aggregate, filter, and transform the data into the right format for training a machine learning model.

## *1. Creating Training Datasets*

The training dataset is used to **train the model**, so it must include all relevant features and target labels. In many cases, the target variable (such as **churn**) needs to be calculated based on certain criteria, and features need to be aggregated and transformed.

Example:

Suppose you are building a model to predict whether a customer will churn based on their behavior, and you want to create a training dataset that includes:

- **Total spent** by the customer.
- **Number of visits** or orders made.
- **Whether the customer has churned** (target variable).

The following SQL query can prepare this dataset:

```sql
Copy
SELECT c.customer_id,
    COALESCE(SUM(s.amount), 0) AS total_spent,
    COUNT(o.order_id) AS total_orders,
    MAX(o.order_date) AS last_order_date,
    CASE WHEN MAX(o.order_date) < CURRENT_DATE - INTERVAL '6
months' THEN 1 ELSE 0 END AS churn
FROM customers c
LEFT JOIN sales s ON c.customer_id = s.customer_id
LEFT JOIN orders o ON c.customer_id = o.customer_id
GROUP BY c.customer_id;
```

This query:

- **Aggregates** the total amount spent by the customer.
- Counts the **total number of orders** placed by the customer.
- Uses **CASE** to create a binary target variable for **churn**, where a value of 1 indicates that the customer has not made a purchase in the last 6 months (thus, they have churned).

## 2. Joining Multiple Tables

Often, the data needed for machine learning models resides in multiple tables, and SQL's powerful **JOIN** functionality can be used to combine this data.

Example:

You can join **customer demographic information**, **purchase data**, and **customer support interaction records** to create a comprehensive dataset for predicting churn:

```sql
Copy
SELECT c.customer_id,
    c.age,
    c.gender,
    SUM(s.amount) AS total_spent,
    COUNT(o.order_id) AS total_orders,
    CASE WHEN MAX(o.order_date) < CURRENT_DATE - INTERVAL '6 months' THEN 1 ELSE 0 END AS churn
FROM customers c
LEFT JOIN sales s ON c.customer_id = s.customer_id
LEFT JOIN orders o ON c.customer_id = o.customer_id
LEFT JOIN customer_support cs ON c.customer_id = cs.customer_id
GROUP BY c.customer_id, c.age, c.gender;
```

In this example, we are pulling data from the **customers** table, **sales** table, **orders** table, and **customer_support** table to build a richer feature set for training a churn prediction model.

---

## Real-World Example: Preparing Customer Behavior Data for a Machine Learning Model in a Marketing Campaign

Let's walk through a real-world example where we use SQL to prepare **customer behavior data** for a marketing campaign machine learning model. The goal is to predict which customers are most likely to respond to a targeted marketing campaign based on their past behavior.

### Step 1: Define the Data Schema

We'll assume we have the following tables:

- **customers**: Contains customer details (customer_id, age, gender, region).
- **sales**: Contains sales data (customer_id, product_id, amount, sale_date).
- **campaign_responses**: Contains data on whether a customer responded to a previous campaign (customer_id, response).

### Step 2: Querying Data for Training

To build our model, we'll need to create a dataset with features such as:

- **Total sales** over the past 6 months.
- **Number of visits** to the website (or orders placed).
- **Response to previous campaigns** (target variable: 1 = Responded, 0 = Did not respond).

We can use the following SQL query to aggregate this data:

```sql
Copy
SELECT c.customer_id,
```

```
c.age,
c.gender,
SUM(s.amount) AS total_spent_last_6_months,
COUNT(o.order_id) AS total_orders_last_6_months,
MAX(o.order_date) AS last_order_date,
CASE WHEN MAX(r.response_date) IS NOT NULL THEN 1 ELSE 0 END
AS responded_to_previous_campaign
FROM customers c
LEFT JOIN sales s ON c.customer_id = s.customer_id
LEFT JOIN orders o ON c.customer_id = o.customer_id
LEFT JOIN campaign_responses r ON c.customer_id = r.customer_id
WHERE o.order_date >= CURRENT_DATE - INTERVAL '6 months'
GROUP BY c.customer_id, c.age, c.gender;
```

This query:

- **Aggregates sales** to calculate the **total_spent_last_6_months**.
- **Counts orders** to calculate **total_orders_last_6_months**.
- **Determines if the customer responded** to a previous campaign, creating a **binary target variable** (1 for response, 0 for no response).

### *Step 3: Loading the Data into Python for Modeling*

After querying the data, we load it into a Python dataframe for machine learning model training:

```python
Copy
import pandas as pd
```

```python
from sqlalchemy import create_engine

# Establish connection to the database
engine =
create_engine('postgresql://username:password@localhost:5432/mydatabase')

# SQL query to extract the data
query = """
SELECT c.customer_id,
    c.age,
    c.gender,
    SUM(s.amount) AS total_spent_last_6_months,
    COUNT(o.order_id) AS total_orders_last_6_months,
    MAX(o.order_date) AS last_order_date,
    CASE WHEN MAX(r.response_date) IS NOT NULL THEN 1 ELSE 0 END
AS responded_to_previous_campaign
FROM customers c
LEFT JOIN sales s ON c.customer_id = s.customer_id
LEFT JOIN orders o ON c.customer_id = o.customer_id
LEFT JOIN campaign_responses r ON c.customer_id = r.customer_id
WHERE o.order_date >= CURRENT_DATE - INTERVAL '6 months'
GROUP BY c.customer_id, c.age, c.gender;
"""

# Load the data into a pandas dataframe
df = pd.read_sql(query, engine)

# Display the dataframe
print(df.head())
```

### *Step 4: Building and Evaluating the Model*

Now, we can split the data into features and target variables, and train a machine learning model (e.g., **Logistic Regression**) to predict the likelihood of customer response to future marketing campaigns.

python
Copy

```python
from sklearn.model_selection import train_test_split
from sklearn.linear_model import LogisticRegression
from sklearn.metrics import accuracy_score

# Features and target variable
X = df[['age', 'gender', 'total_spent_last_6_months', 'total_orders_last_6_months']]
y = df['responded_to_previous_campaign']

# Split the data into training and testing sets
X_train, X_test, y_train, y_test = train_test_split(X, y, test_size=0.3, random_state=42)

# Train a logistic regression model
model = LogisticRegression()
model.fit(X_train, y_train)

# Make predictions and evaluate the model
y_pred = model.predict(X_test)
print(f'Model Accuracy: {accuracy_score(y_test, y_pred)}')
```

In this chapter, we explored how to **integrate SQL with machine learning workflows**, focusing on using SQL for:

- **Data preparation**: Extracting, cleaning, and transforming data for machine learning models.
- **Complex SQL queries**: Using SQL to extract meaningful features and target variables for training models.
- A **real-world example** of preparing **customer behavior data** for a **marketing campaign** machine learning model.

SQL is an essential tool in data science for preparing and extracting data from relational databases, and it can be seamlessly integrated with Python or R for building machine learning models. In the next chapter, we will discuss **advanced machine learning techniques** and how to optimize models for better performance.

# Chapter 23: Advanced SQL for Big Data

As data continues to grow exponentially, traditional relational databases often struggle to handle the large-scale data required for advanced analytics. Big data platforms such as **Apache Hive**, **Google BigQuery**, and **Amazon Redshift** have emerged to provide scalable solutions for storing, querying, and analyzing massive datasets. This chapter will explore how to use **SQL** with these big data platforms, focusing on **query optimization** and best practices for large-scale datasets. We will also walk through a **real-world example** of running SQL queries on a massive dataset to analyze **user behavior** across multiple regions.

## Introduction to SQL for Big Data Platforms

Big data platforms are designed to handle, store, and process datasets that are far too large to fit into a single machine or traditional database. These platforms allow data scientists, analysts, and engineers to work with datasets that consist of petabytes of data, all while ensuring scalability and performance.

### 1. Apache Hive

**Apache Hive** is a data warehouse system built on top of **Apache Hadoop**, which is a popular framework for distributed storage and processing of large datasets. Hive uses a SQL-like language called

**HiveQL**, which makes it easy for users familiar with SQL to interact with big data stored in Hadoop Distributed File System (HDFS).

**Key Features of Hive:**

- **SQL-like querying**: Hive uses HiveQL, which is similar to SQL and supports complex queries.
- **Scalability**: Hive is built on top of Hadoop, which can scale to handle petabytes of data.
- **Integration with Hadoop**: Hive leverages Hadoop's distributed computing capabilities for query execution.

**Example:**

Hive can be used to query data stored in HDFS. For example, querying a large dataset of user activity logs:

```sql
Copy
SELECT user_id, COUNT(*) AS activities_count
FROM user_activity_logs
WHERE region = 'US'
GROUP BY user_id;
```

This query aggregates user activity logs for users in the "US" region, counting the number of activities each user has performed.

## 2. Google BigQuery

**Google BigQuery** is a fully managed, serverless, and highly scalable data warehouse solution provided by Google Cloud. It enables users to analyze large datasets using **SQL** without the need to manage infrastructure or clusters. BigQuery is designed for fast SQL queries on large-scale datasets, and it's optimized for performing analytics on big data in real time.

## Key Features of BigQuery:

- **Serverless**: No need to manage infrastructure; BigQuery scales automatically as the dataset grows.
- **Massive scalability**: BigQuery is designed to handle petabytes of data efficiently.
- **Real-time analytics**: BigQuery supports real-time data analysis and provides sub-second query response times.

## Example:

Running a query on a massive user dataset in BigQuery:

```sql
Copy
SELECT user_id, COUNT(*) AS activity_count
FROM `project_id.dataset_id.user_activity`
WHERE region = 'EU'
GROUP BY user_id;
```

This query counts the number of activities per user in the **EU** region using the **user_activity** table stored in BigQuery.

### 3. Amazon Redshift

**Amazon Redshift** is a fully managed data warehouse service by Amazon Web Services (AWS). It allows users to run large-scale data analytics on structured data using SQL. Redshift uses a distributed architecture to provide high performance and scalability for data analysis.

## Key Features of Redshift:

- **Columnar storage**: Redshift uses columnar storage, which optimizes read-heavy query performance and is ideal for analytics.
- **Massively Parallel Processing (MPP)**: Redshift distributes data across multiple nodes, enabling parallel processing for faster query execution.
- **Integration with AWS**: Redshift integrates seamlessly with other AWS services, such as **S3**, **Kinesis**, and **EMR**.

## Example:

Querying data on user behavior in Redshift:

```sql
Copy
SELECT user_id, SUM(purchase_amount) AS total_spent
FROM sales_data
WHERE region = 'Asia'
GROUP BY user_id;
```

This query calculates the total amount spent by each user in the **Asia** region, utilizing Redshift's distributed query execution for performance optimization.

---

## Optimizing Queries for Large-Scale Datasets

Working with large datasets requires optimizing SQL queries to ensure that they run efficiently and don't consume excessive resources. Below are some key techniques for optimizing SQL queries in big data platforms:

### 1. Partitioning and Sharding

Partitioning refers to dividing large tables into smaller, more manageable pieces. In big data platforms, **partitioning** is often based on a column like **date** or **region**.

- **Partitioning** divides large tables into smaller segments, improving performance by allowing queries to scan only the relevant partitions.
- **Sharding** distributes data across multiple servers or nodes.

Example:

In **Google BigQuery**, partitioning data by date improves query performance when filtering by date range.

sql

Copy
```
CREATE TABLE user_activity_partitioned
PARTITION BY DATE(activity_date)
AS
SELECT * FROM user_activity;
```

## 2. Using Indexes

Indexes can dramatically speed up query performance by reducing the amount of data the database needs to scan. While big data platforms like **Hive** and **Redshift** do not support traditional indexing in the same way as relational databases, they use other techniques like **sorting**, **distribution keys**, and **materialized views**.

- **Sorting**: Sorting large datasets on frequently queried columns speeds up read operations.
- **Distribution Keys**: In Amazon Redshift, choosing appropriate distribution keys helps distribute data evenly across nodes, reducing the need for data shuffling.

## 3. Query Aggregation and Filtering

- **Pushdown Filters**: Big data platforms like **BigQuery** and **Redshift** automatically push filter conditions (e.g., WHERE clauses) down to the data storage layer, reducing the amount of data processed.
- **Avoiding SELECT * Queries**: Always specify only the columns you need in your queries to reduce the data load.

## *4. Data Compression*

Many big data platforms support **data compression**, which helps reduce storage space and speeds up data retrieval. Compressed data can be queried more efficiently, especially in columnar storage databases like **Redshift**.

---

# Real-World Example: Running SQL Queries on a Massive Dataset to Analyze User Behavior Across Multiple Regions

Let's walk through a practical example of using SQL on a large-scale dataset to analyze **user behavior** across multiple regions. Suppose we have a **user_activity** table that contains millions of records, and we want to analyze the behavior of users across three regions: **North America**, **Europe**, and **Asia**.

### *Step 1: Extracting the Relevant Data*

First, we will extract the relevant data from the **user_activity** table by grouping users based on their **region** and calculating metrics like the **total activity count** and **average session duration**.

Example Query:

```sql
Copy
SELECT region,
    COUNT(user_id) AS total_users,
    SUM(session_duration) AS total_duration,
```

AVG(session_duration) AS avg_duration
FROM user_activity
WHERE activity_date BETWEEN '2023-01-01' AND '2023-12-31'
GROUP BY region;

This query:

- Filters the **user_activity** data to include only activities from the year 2023.
- Groups the data by **region** (North America, Europe, Asia).
- Aggregates the total number of users, total session duration, and average session duration per region.

### Step 2: Optimizing the Query for Big Data

Given that this query runs on a massive dataset, it is important to optimize it:

- **Partition the data** by **activity_date** and **region** to speed up filtering and aggregation.
- Use **distribution keys** (in Redshift) or **clustering keys** (in Hive) to evenly distribute the data.

### Step 3: Analyzing the Data

The results of the query might look like this:

| region | total_users | total_duration | avg_duration |
|---|---|---|---|
| North America | 500,000 | 50,000,000 | 100 |

| region | total_users | total_duration | avg_duration |
|--------|-------------|----------------|--------------|
| Europe | 300,000 | 25,000,000 | 83.33 |
| Asia | 700,000 | 70,000,000 | 100 |

From this table, we can analyze user behavior across regions. For instance, **North America** and **Asia** have similar average session durations, while **Europe** has a slightly lower average duration.

### *Step 4: Further Analysis and Machine Learning Preparation*

Once the data is aggregated, it can be fed into a machine learning model to predict user engagement based on features such as **session duration** and **region**. This aggregated data can be used for deeper analysis, such as:

- Predicting which regions are more likely to engage with a new feature.
- Segmenting users for personalized marketing campaigns based on activity levels.

In this chapter, we covered how SQL can be used in **big data platforms** like **Apache Hive**, **Google BigQuery**, and **Amazon Redshift** to analyze large datasets. Key concepts included:

- **Partitioning**, **indexing**, and **compression** techniques for optimizing queries.
- **SQL query optimization** for working with massive datasets.
- A **real-world example** of running SQL queries to analyze **user behavior** across multiple regions.

SQL is a powerful tool that can be seamlessly integrated into big data workflows to extract insights from large datasets. As data continues to grow, mastering SQL in big data platforms will be crucial for data scientists and analysts.

In the next chapter, we will explore **SQL for Data Integration**, focusing on how to combine data from multiple sources for unified analysis and reporting.

# Chapter 24: Using SQL for Data Visualization

Data visualization is a crucial step in the data analysis process, enabling you to communicate insights in a clear and effective manner. SQL plays a vital role in this process by helping you query and prepare the data needed for visualizations. In this chapter, we will explore how to:

- Use SQL to query data for visualization.
- Integrate SQL with popular data visualization tools like **Tableau, Power BI**, and **matplotlib**.
- Walk through a **real-world example** of querying and visualizing **sales data** using **Tableau**.

---

## Querying Data for Use in Visualizations

Before visualizing data, you must first prepare it through querying. SQL helps you extract and aggregate the relevant data, often performing operations like filtering, grouping, and joining tables, so it is in the right format for analysis and visualization.

### *1. Aggregating Data for Visualizations*

Most visualizations require aggregated data, such as sums, averages, or counts, to provide useful insights. SQL provides powerful aggregation functions like **SUM**, **AVG**, **COUNT**, and **MAX** to calculate metrics, which can then be plotted as graphs.

### Example: Querying Total Sales by Month

Suppose we have a **sales** table with the following columns:

- **sale_id** (unique identifier for the sale).
- **sale_date** (the date the sale occurred).
- **sale_amount** (the value of the sale).

To visualize monthly sales trends, we need to aggregate sales data by month and year:

sql
Copy
```
SELECT
    EXTRACT(YEAR FROM sale_date) AS year,
    EXTRACT(MONTH FROM sale_date) AS month,
    SUM(sale_amount) AS total_sales
FROM sales
GROUP BY year, month
ORDER BY year, month;
```
This query:

- Extracts the **year** and **month** from the **sale_date**.
- Sums the **sale_amount** for each month, aggregating sales data.

- Orders the results by **year** and **month**, which is ideal for visualizing sales over time.

## 2. Filtering Data for Visualizations

Often, you only want to visualize a subset of your data. SQL allows you to filter the data using the **WHERE** clause.

Example: Filtering Sales Data for a Specific Product

If we only want to visualize the sales data for a specific product category, we can add a filter:

```sql
Copy
SELECT
    EXTRACT(YEAR FROM sale_date) AS year,
    EXTRACT(MONTH FROM sale_date) AS month,
    SUM(sale_amount) AS total_sales
FROM sales
WHERE product_category = 'Electronics'
GROUP BY year, month
ORDER BY year, month;
```

This query filters sales data to include only the **Electronics** category.

## 3. Joining Tables for Richer Data

Often, your visualizations will require data from multiple tables. SQL's **JOIN** operations allow you to combine data from different tables. For example, you might want to visualize sales along with customer demographics, so you need to join the **sales** table with a **customers** table.

**Example: Sales by Customer Region**

sql

Copy

```
SELECT
    c.region,
    EXTRACT(YEAR FROM s.sale_date) AS year,
    EXTRACT(MONTH FROM s.sale_date) AS month,
    SUM(s.sale_amount) AS total_sales
FROM sales s
JOIN customers c ON s.customer_id = c.customer_id
GROUP BY c.region, year, month
ORDER BY c.region, year, month;
```

This query joins the **sales** and **customers** tables on **customer_id**, aggregates sales by **region**, and extracts year and month. The resulting data can be visualized to compare sales performance across different regions.

---

## Integrating SQL with Data Visualization Tools

Many data visualization tools allow you to directly connect to SQL databases and run queries to pull data for visualization. Some of the most popular tools include **Tableau**, **Power BI**, and **matplotlib** (for Python). Let's explore how SQL can be integrated with each of these tools to create powerful visualizations.

### *1. Integrating SQL with Tableau*

**Tableau** is a popular data visualization tool that connects directly to various data sources, including SQL databases. You can use Tableau's built-in **SQL connector** to query data directly from a relational database and visualize it interactively.

Steps to Use SQL in Tableau:

1. **Connect to the Data Source**: Open Tableau and select the **SQL database** you want to connect to (e.g., MySQL, PostgreSQL, or Redshift).

2. **Write SQL Queries**: In the data connection window, Tableau allows you to write custom SQL queries to retrieve the data you need.

3. **Build Visualizations**: Once the data is loaded, you can use Tableau's drag-and-drop interface to create charts, graphs, and dashboards.

Real-World Example: Visualizing Sales Trends

To visualize **monthly sales trends** in Tableau, you can write the following SQL query (as shown earlier) to aggregate sales by month and year:

```sql
Copy
SELECT
    EXTRACT(YEAR FROM sale_date) AS year,
    EXTRACT(MONTH FROM sale_date) AS month,
    SUM(sale_amount) AS total_sales
```

FROM sales

GROUP BY year, month

ORDER BY year, month;

Once the data is loaded into Tableau, you can create a **line chart** to show sales over time, or a **bar chart** to compare monthly sales.

## 2. Integrating SQL with Power BI

**Power BI** is another widely used business intelligence and data visualization tool. Similar to Tableau, Power BI allows you to connect to SQL databases and write custom SQL queries to pull the necessary data.

### Steps to Use SQL in Power BI:

1. **Connect to the Data Source**: In Power BI, click on **Get Data** and select the appropriate **SQL database** connector (e.g., SQL Server).

2. **Write SQL Queries**: Power BI lets you enter custom SQL queries to pull specific datasets.

3. **Build Reports**: Once the data is loaded, use Power BI's features to create charts, graphs, and dashboards.

### Real-World Example: Visualizing Sales by Region

You can query **sales data** by **region** as shown in the previous section and load it into Power BI. Once the data is available, you can create a **map visualization** to show sales across different geographic regions, or a **bar chart** to compare sales performance between regions.

### 3. Integrating SQL with Matplotlib (Python)

For more programmatic control over your visualizations, **matplotlib** (a popular Python library) can be used in combination with **pandas** to visualize SQL query results. You can query data from SQL, load it into a pandas dataframe, and then use matplotlib to create custom plots.

Steps to Use SQL in Python (matplotlib):

1. **Connect to the Database**: Use **SQLAlchemy** or **pandas** to connect to the SQL database.
2. **Run SQL Queries**: Use **pandas'** read_sql() function to execute SQL queries and load the data into a dataframe.
3. **Create Visualizations**: Use **matplotlib** to generate plots based on the data.

Example: Visualizing Sales Trends with Matplotlib

python
Copy

```python
import pandas as pd
import matplotlib.pyplot as plt
from sqlalchemy import create_engine

# Establish connection to the database
```

```
engine                                                                    =
create_engine('postgresql://username:password@localhost:5432/mydatabase')

# Run SQL query to extract sales data
query = """
SELECT
    EXTRACT(YEAR FROM sale_date) AS year,
    EXTRACT(MONTH FROM sale_date) AS month,
    SUM(sale_amount) AS total_sales
FROM sales
GROUP BY year, month
ORDER BY year, month;
"""

# Load the query result into a pandas dataframe
df = pd.read_sql(query, engine)

# Create a line plot using matplotlib
plt.plot(df['month'], df['total_sales'])
plt.title('Monthly Sales Trends')
plt.xlabel('Month')
plt.ylabel('Total Sales')
plt.xticks(df['month'])
plt.show()
```

This Python code uses SQL to extract **monthly sales data,** loads it into a pandas dataframe, and visualizes the data using **matplotlib.**

# Real-World Example: Querying and Visualizing Sales Data Using Tableau

Let's take a deeper dive into how we can **query and visualize sales data** in **Tableau**. In this scenario, we are analyzing **sales performance** across different **regions** for the past year.

### *Step 1: Query the Data*

Write the SQL query to retrieve the necessary data:

```sql
Copy
SELECT
    region,
    EXTRACT(YEAR FROM sale_date) AS year,
    SUM(sale_amount) AS total_sales
FROM sales
WHERE sale_date >= '2023-01-01'
GROUP BY region, year
ORDER BY region, year;
```

This query aggregates sales by **region** and **year**, filtering for sales that occurred in **2023**.

### *Step 2: Load the Data into Tableau*

Once the data is loaded into Tableau, you can use the **drag-and-drop** interface to create a **bar chart** comparing total sales across regions for the year 2023.

- Drag **region** to the **Columns** shelf.

- Drag **total_sales** to the **Rows** shelf.
- Use **year** to create a **filter** or to group sales by year.

***Step 3: Visualize the Data***

Tableau will generate a bar chart showing sales per region. You can customize the chart further by changing the **color** or **formatting** to make the insights clearer.

---

In this chapter, we covered the integration of **SQL** with **data visualization** tools like **Tableau**, **Power BI**, and **matplotlib**. We:

- Learned how to query and aggregate data with SQL to prepare it for visualization.
- Explored how to integrate SQL with data visualization tools for creating interactive and informative visualizations.
- Walked through a **real-world example** of visualizing **sales data** using **Tableau**, and discussed the steps involved in extracting, transforming, and visualizing the data.

SQL serves as a powerful tool for data preparation, while visualization tools like Tableau and Power BI allow users to present the data in a more accessible and insightful manner. In the next chapter, we will discuss **SQL for Data Security and Compliance**, focusing on how to secure and manage data in SQL databases.

# Chapter 25: Troubleshooting and Debugging SQL Queries

SQL is a powerful tool for managing and analyzing data, but as with any programming language, errors and issues can arise when writing queries. In this chapter, we will focus on how to troubleshoot and debug SQL queries effectively. You will learn to identify common errors, debug queries, and apply techniques to fix issues. We will conclude with a **real-world example** of troubleshooting a query that joins multiple tables and returns incorrect results.

---

## Common Errors in SQL Queries and How to Fix Them

SQL queries can fail for various reasons, including syntax issues, logic errors, and problems with data types. Below are some of the most common SQL errors and their solutions:

### 1. Syntax Errors

- **Error**: This is the most common type of error. It happens when SQL syntax is incorrect.
- **Example**: Forgetting to close a parenthesis or missing a comma between fields.

sql

Copy

SELECT name, age FROM users WHERE age > 30;

In this query, a missing **FROM** clause or a forgotten comma between fields could result in a syntax error.

Fix: Ensure that you follow the correct syntax for SQL statements, including appropriate use of commas, parentheses, and keywords.

## 2. *Incorrect JOINs*

- **Error**: When joining multiple tables, missing or incorrectly using the **ON** condition can lead to incorrect or missing results. For example, missing the join condition may cause a **Cartesian product** (every row in the first table is joined with every row in the second table).

sql

Copy

```sql
SELECT employees.name, departments.department_name
FROM employees
JOIN departments;
```

Fix: Ensure that you specify the correct join conditions using the ON clause to match records between the tables.

sql

Copy

```sql
SELECT employees.name, departments.department_name
FROM employees
```

JOIN departments ON employees.department_id = departments.department_id;

## 3. Data Type Mismatch

- **Error**: Using incompatible data types in SQL operations (e.g., trying to compare a string with a number) can lead to errors.

sql

Copy

```
SELECT * FROM users WHERE user_id = 'string_value';
```

Fix: Ensure that the data types of the columns match the values being compared. If necessary, use CAST or CONVERT to convert data types.

sql

Copy

```
SELECT * FROM users WHERE user_id = CAST('string_value' AS INT);
```

## 4. Missing or Incorrect Group By Clauses

- **Error**: In aggregate queries, forgetting to group data properly can lead to errors or incorrect results.

sql

Copy

```
SELECT department, COUNT(*) FROM employees;
```

This query will return an error because we are aggregating data (counting employees) but not grouping by department.

Fix: Ensure that you use GROUP BY when aggregating data.

sql

Copy

```
SELECT department, COUNT(*) FROM employees
GROUP BY department;
```

## 5. Subquery Issues

- **Error**: Subqueries can sometimes be improperly structured, leading to errors or unexpected results.

sql

Copy

```
SELECT name FROM employees WHERE department_id IN (SELECT department_id FROM departments);
```

This query will throw an error if the subquery returns more than one column, which is not allowed in an **IN** clause.

Fix: Ensure that subqueries return the correct number of columns for the clause that is being used.

sql

Copy

```
SELECT name FROM employees WHERE department_id IN (SELECT department_id FROM departments WHERE active = 1);
```

# Debugging Techniques to Identify Issues with SQL Queries

When a query doesn't return the expected results, debugging is necessary. Here are a few effective debugging techniques:

## 1. Break Down Complex Queries

When dealing with complex queries, break the query down into smaller parts and test each part individually. This will help identify the part of the query that is causing the issue.

Example:

If a query is joining multiple tables and returning incorrect results, test the **individual joins** first to ensure each one is working correctly.

sql
Copy
```
SELECT * FROM employees;
SELECT * FROM departments;
SELECT * FROM employees JOIN departments ON employees.department_id =
departments.department_id;
```
By running each part separately, you can isolate the problem.

## 2. Use EXPLAIN to Analyze Query Execution

Many databases provide an **EXPLAIN** command that shows the execution plan of a query. This can help identify inefficient joins, missing indexes, and other performance issues.

Example:
sql
Copy
```
EXPLAIN SELECT name FROM employees WHERE department_id = 1;
```

The output will show you how the database is executing the query, including whether it's using indexes and how it's scanning tables.

### 3. Check for NULL Values

NULL values can lead to incorrect results or no results at all, especially when comparing values. Ensure that you account for **NULL** in your queries using **IS NULL** or **COALESCE**.

Example:

sql

Copy

```
SELECT name FROM employees WHERE department_id IS NULL;
```

### 4. Test with Smaller Datasets

If your query is returning too many results or causing performance issues, test it on a smaller subset of the data (e.g., limit the number of rows returned or filter by date range) to see if the issue persists.

sql

Copy

```
SELECT name FROM employees LIMIT 10;
```

Testing with smaller datasets helps quickly identify whether the issue is related to data volume or query logic.

### 5. Use Aggregate Functions for Debugging

For troubleshooting issues related to aggregations (e.g., **COUNT, SUM, AVG**), it's often helpful to check if the aggregations are happening correctly by including more detail.

**Example:**

If the **COUNT** function is not working as expected, try adding more columns to understand the distribution of data:

```sql
sql
Copy
SELECT department_id, COUNT(*), MAX(salary), MIN(salary)
FROM employees
GROUP BY department_id;
```

This query provides more information about the distribution of salaries in each department, which can help you spot errors in the aggregation.

---

## Real-World Example: Troubleshooting a Query that Joins Multiple Tables and Returns Incorrect Results

Let's go through an example where we troubleshoot a query that joins multiple tables and returns incorrect results. Imagine we have the following tables:

- **employees**: Stores employee data (employee_id, name, department_id, salary).
- **departments**: Stores department data (department_id, department_name).
- **salaries**: Stores salary data (employee_id, salary, effective_date).

The goal is to find out the **average salary** of employees by department, but the query is returning incorrect results.

sql

Copy

```
SELECT d.department_name, AVG(s.salary) AS avg_salary
FROM employees e
JOIN departments d ON e.department_id = d.department_id
JOIN salaries s ON e.employee_id = s.employee_id
GROUP BY d.department_name;
```

The query seems to return the **average salary** for each department, but it's incorrect. The issue might be caused by multiple entries in the **salaries** table for each employee (e.g., they have salary records over time).

### Step 1: Check the Data

Start by checking if the **salaries** table contains multiple records for each employee. For example, the same employee may have multiple salary records for different time periods.

sql

Copy

```
SELECT employee_id, COUNT(*) FROM salaries GROUP BY employee_id;
```

If the result shows that some employees have multiple salary records, this is likely the cause of the issue.

### Step 2: Fix the Query

To fix this, we need to ensure that we only use the most recent salary record for each employee. We can do this by using the **ROW_NUMBER** window function to rank the salary records and select only the most recent record for each employee.

sql
Copy

```
WITH latest_salaries AS (
    SELECT employee_id, salary, department_id,
        ROW_NUMBER() OVER (PARTITION BY employee_id ORDER BY effective_date DESC) AS rank
    FROM salaries
)
SELECT d.department_name, AVG(ls.salary) AS avg_salary
FROM employees e
JOIN departments d ON e.department_id = d.department_id
JOIN latest_salaries ls ON e.employee_id = ls.employee_id AND ls.rank = 1
GROUP BY d.department_name;
```

In this query:

- We use a **CTE (Common Table Expression)** with **ROW_NUMBER** to rank salary records for each employee by **effective_date** in descending order.
- We then select only the most recent salary record by filtering on **rank = 1**.

### Step 3: Verify the Results

Run the query again to check if the results are now correct. The query should return the accurate **average salary** per department, using only the most recent salary record for each employee.

---

In this chapter, we covered:

- Common SQL errors, such as syntax mistakes, incorrect joins, data type mismatches, and issues with aggregations.
- Techniques for debugging SQL queries, including breaking down complex queries, using **EXPLAIN** for query optimization, and checking for **NULL** values.
- A **real-world example** of troubleshooting a query that joins multiple tables and returns incorrect results, and how to fix it using window functions and **ROW_NUMBER**.

Debugging SQL queries is an essential skill for anyone working with databases, and understanding how to troubleshoot and optimize your queries can save you time and help you deliver more accurate results.

In the next chapter, we will explore **SQL for Advanced Data Modeling**, focusing on more complex data relationships and advanced database design techniques.

# Chapter 26: Building Reusable SQL Queries for Data Science

As data science projects often require repeated querying and analysis of the same datasets, it is essential to write **efficient**, **reusable** SQL queries that can be easily maintained and executed. This chapter will focus on how to:

- Write **efficient, reusable SQL queries** for reporting and data analysis.
- Create **views** and **stored procedures** to encapsulate SQL logic, making it more modular and easier to maintain.
- Walk through a **real-world example** of creating a set of views to regularly monitor **business KPIs** in an organization.

---

## Writing Efficient, Reusable SQL Queries for Reporting and Data Analysis

When working on data analysis and reporting tasks, it's common to run similar queries repeatedly to fetch specific metrics, such as sales, customer activity, or financial data. Writing efficient and reusable SQL queries ensures that you don't have to rewrite complex logic each time and helps keep your queries modular and scalable.

## *1. Avoiding Repetition in Queries*

One of the best practices for writing reusable SQL queries is to avoid redundancy. For example, instead of copying the same complex JOIN operations, aggregation logic, and filtering conditions in each query, we can create reusable components such as **views** or **common table expressions (CTEs)**.

Example:

Imagine you are analyzing sales data and need to calculate **total sales by region** every month. Instead of repeatedly writing the same JOIN and aggregation logic, you can create a **view** that encapsulates this logic.

```sql
Copy
CREATE VIEW sales_by_region AS
SELECT region,
    EXTRACT(YEAR FROM sale_date) AS year,
    EXTRACT(MONTH FROM sale_date) AS month,
    SUM(sale_amount) AS total_sales
FROM sales
GROUP BY region, year, month;
```

With the **view** in place, you can now simply query the sales_by_region view whenever you need the data.

```sql
Copy
SELECT * FROM sales_by_region WHERE region = 'North America';
```

This approach avoids repetition, ensures consistency in reporting, and makes the logic easier to maintain.

## 2. Using Joins and Subqueries Effectively

When creating reusable queries for reporting, it's crucial to write queries that can efficiently combine data from multiple tables using **joins** or **subqueries**. These operations allow you to link datasets together to answer more complex business questions.

For example, if you need to calculate the **total sales per customer** across multiple sales transactions, you could write the following query that joins the **sales** and **customers** tables:

sql
Copy
```
SELECT c.customer_id,
    c.customer_name,
    SUM(s.sale_amount) AS total_sales
FROM customers c
JOIN sales s ON c.customer_id = s.customer_id
GROUP BY c.customer_id, c.customer_name;
```
By using **JOINs** effectively, you can combine data from different tables and return comprehensive insights in a single query.

## 3. Using Aggregate Functions for Reusability

Many data analysis queries involve **aggregation** functions like **SUM, AVG, COUNT**, and **MAX**. These functions are often used repeatedly in reports to summarize data.

To avoid redundant logic, you can encapsulate aggregate functions into **views** or **CTEs** for easy reuse.

Example:

You might frequently need to calculate the **average sales per product**. Instead of writing this logic each time, you can create a **view**:

sql
Copy
```
CREATE VIEW avg_sales_per_product AS
SELECT product_id,
    AVG(sale_amount) AS avg_sale
FROM sales
GROUP BY product_id;
```
Now, you can easily retrieve the average sales for any product with a simple query:

sql
Copy
```
SELECT * FROM avg_sales_per_product WHERE product_id = 101;
```
This is a reusable, efficient way to handle repeated aggregation logic.

## Creating Views and Stored Procedures to Encapsulate SQL Logic

SQL **views** and **stored procedures** are two powerful tools that allow you to encapsulate complex SQL logic and make your queries reusable and easier to maintain.

## 1. Views

A **view** is a virtual table that encapsulates the results of a SQL query. Views simplify complex queries by abstracting away the logic from the end user. They are particularly useful for frequently used queries or when you want to hide complex logic from users who query the database.

### Creating a View:

You can create a view by writing a **SELECT** query and storing it in the database with a CREATE VIEW statement.

```sql
Copy
CREATE VIEW employee_sales AS
SELECT e.employee_id,
    e.employee_name,
    SUM(s.sale_amount) AS total_sales
FROM employees e
JOIN sales s ON e.employee_id = s.employee_id
GROUP BY e.employee_id, e.employee_name;
```

This view combines employee and sales data into a **virtual table** that can be queried just like any other table in the database.

### Querying a View:

Once the view is created, you can query it directly:

sql

Copy

SELECT * FROM employee_sales WHERE total_sales > 10000;

This simplifies reporting and analysis, as users can focus on querying the view rather than constructing complex SQL logic each time.

## 2. Stored Procedures

A **stored procedure** is a set of SQL statements that can be executed on demand. Stored procedures are particularly useful for encapsulating business logic that needs to be reused multiple times. Unlike views, stored procedures can accept **parameters**, which makes them flexible for use in different scenarios.

### Creating a Stored Procedure:

Here's an example of a stored procedure that calculates the **total sales** for a given **region** and **year**:

sql

Copy

```
CREATE PROCEDURE GetTotalSalesByRegionAndYear(IN input_region
VARCHAR(255), IN input_year INT)
BEGIN
    SELECT region,
        SUM(sale_amount) AS total_sales
    FROM sales
    WHERE region = input_region
        AND EXTRACT(YEAR FROM sale_date) = input_year
    GROUP BY region;
```

END;

Calling a Stored Procedure:

To run the stored procedure, simply call it with the appropriate parameters:

```sql
Copy
CALL GetTotalSalesByRegionAndYear('North America', 2023);
```

This stored procedure can be reused for any region and year, making it an efficient way to encapsulate and reuse SQL logic.

---

## Real-World Example: Creating a Set of Views to Regularly Monitor Business KPIs in an Organization

Let's say you are tasked with building a set of views to monitor **Key Performance Indicators (KPIs)** regularly for a business. These KPIs include:

- **Total sales by region**.
- **Average sales per employee**.
- **Customer churn rate**.

You can create **views** to encapsulate these queries, making it easy for business analysts and stakeholders to query the KPIs without having to re-run complex queries every time.

### *Step 1: Create a View for Total Sales by Region*

sql

Copy

```sql
CREATE VIEW total_sales_by_region AS
SELECT region,
    SUM(sale_amount) AS total_sales
FROM sales
GROUP BY region;
```

This view will allow you to quickly retrieve total sales by region with a simple query:

sql

Copy

```sql
SELECT * FROM total_sales_by_region;
```

### *Step 2: Create a View for Average Sales per Employee*

sql

Copy

```sql
CREATE VIEW avg_sales_per_employee AS
SELECT employee_id,
    AVG(sale_amount) AS avg_sale
FROM sales
GROUP BY employee_id;
```

With this view, you can easily get the average sales per employee:

sql

Copy

```sql
SELECT * FROM avg_sales_per_employee WHERE employee_id = 101;
```

### *Step 3: Create a View for Customer Churn Rate*

Customer churn can be calculated based on the number of customers who have not made any purchases in a certain time period. Here's how to create a view for **customer churn rate**:

sql
Copy
```
CREATE VIEW customer_churn_rate AS
SELECT
    COUNT(DISTINCT CASE WHEN MAX(sale_date) < CURRENT_DATE -
INTERVAL '6 months' THEN customer_id END)
    / COUNT(DISTINCT customer_id) AS churn_rate
FROM customers c
LEFT JOIN sales s ON c.customer_id = s.customer_id;
```

This view calculates the churn rate by counting customers who have not made purchases in the last 6 months and dividing it by the total number of customers.

### *Step 4: Querying the Views for Business Monitoring*

Now, using these views, the business can easily monitor key metrics like total sales, average sales per employee, and churn rate without the need to rewrite SQL queries. For example, querying total sales by region:

sql
Copy
```
SELECT * FROM total_sales_by_region;
```

This allows for easy **real-time monitoring** and decision-making based on **KPIs**.

In this chapter, we discussed how to:

- Write **efficient, reusable SQL queries** for reporting and data analysis by using views and stored procedures.
- Create **views** to encapsulate complex SQL logic and provide reusable query structures.
- Write **stored procedures** for flexible, parameterized SQL logic that can be invoked multiple times with different inputs.

Through a **real-world example**, we demonstrated how to create a set of views to regularly monitor **business KPIs** in an organization, enabling better decision-making and improving the efficiency of reporting processes.

In the next chapter, we will explore **SQL for Advanced Data Analytics**, focusing on more complex analytical techniques and how SQL can be used in advanced data science workflows.

# Chapter 27: The Future of SQL and Data Science

SQL has long been the backbone of data querying and analysis, but with the rapid evolution of technologies like **cloud computing**, **big data**, and **machine learning**, SQL's role in data science is transforming. In this final chapter, we will explore the future of SQL in data science, highlighting emerging trends, advancements in query optimization, and the increasing importance of mastering SQL for future projects. We will conclude with insights on how to become an expert SQL user, empowering you to navigate the evolving landscape of data science.

---

## The Evolving Role of SQL in Data Science as New Technologies Emerge

SQL has been the standard for working with relational databases for decades, and its importance remains critical, especially in the realm of **data science**. However, as new technologies emerge, SQL is adapting and integrating with **cloud platforms**, **big data tools**, and **machine learning** workflows.

### 1. SQL in the Cloud

With the advent of cloud computing, traditional on-premise databases are being replaced or integrated with cloud-based platforms like **Amazon Redshift**, **Google BigQuery**, and **Azure SQL Database**. These platforms provide scalability, flexibility, and near-instant provisioning, making them ideal for handling large datasets that data scientists work with today.

**Why SQL is Crucial in the Cloud:**

- **Cloud-native SQL engines**: Tools like BigQuery and Redshift are designed to scale massively and still rely heavily on SQL for querying.
- **Integration with cloud services**: SQL in the cloud works seamlessly with other cloud-native tools for data analysis, visualization, and machine learning.
- **Big data analytics**: SQL remains the preferred querying language for data scientists working with big data stored in cloud platforms, especially for structured data.

As cloud services continue to improve, SQL is expected to remain at the core of data retrieval and management in cloud-based environments.

## 2. SQL for Machine Learning

Machine learning (ML) is becoming an essential part of the data science workflow. SQL's integration with machine learning frameworks is growing, especially as more databases incorporate

**SQL-based machine learning** (e.g., **BigQuery ML, SQL Server Machine Learning Services**).

How SQL and Machine Learning are Integrated:

- **In-database machine learning**: Tools like BigQuery ML allow data scientists to train machine learning models directly within the database using SQL queries. This eliminates the need to export data to external tools.

- **SQL-based data preprocessing**: SQL can be used for **data cleaning, feature engineering**, and **aggregations** in the data preparation stage before feeding the data into machine learning algorithms.

- **Model evaluation and prediction**: Data scientists can use SQL to run predictions on large datasets and evaluate model performance through direct querying of model outputs stored in databases.

In the future, **SQL and machine learning** will become even more tightly integrated, enabling data scientists to perform end-to-end machine learning tasks directly within databases.

---

## Trends in SQL Query Optimization and Big Data

As data science continues to evolve, so do the techniques and technologies for optimizing SQL queries and working with big data. Some of the key trends in SQL query optimization and big data analytics include:

## 1. Big Data and Distributed Querying

Working with massive datasets in **big data environments** (e.g., Hadoop, Spark, and NoSQL databases) requires optimized SQL queries that can scale across distributed systems.

Optimizing Queries for Big Data:

- **Partitioning**: Query performance is often improved by partitioning large datasets into smaller, more manageable chunks.
- **Sharding**: Sharding distributes data across multiple servers, allowing for parallel processing of queries, improving query performance in large datasets.
- **Indexes and materialized views**: In big data platforms like **Apache Hive**, **Redshift**, and **BigQuery**, indexing and creating materialized views can optimize query performance by storing pre-aggregated results or frequently queried data.

## 2. SQL Query Optimization

With large datasets, inefficient queries can become a bottleneck. Optimizing SQL queries is a skill that remains crucial, especially as the volume of data continues to grow.

Trends in Query Optimization:

- **Cost-based optimization**: SQL engines like **PostgreSQL**, **MySQL**, and **BigQuery** are employing cost-based query optimization, which selects the most efficient execution plan for running queries.

- **Parallel execution**: Platforms like **Amazon Redshift** and **Google BigQuery** are leveraging **parallel query execution** to distribute the work across multiple processors, significantly speeding up queries on large datasets.

- **Query refactoring**: Using techniques like **subquery optimization**, **avoidance of SELECT *** (selecting only necessary columns), and **using window functions** over joins can make queries more efficient.

## 3. Data Lakes and SQL

As organizations store more unstructured data in **data lakes**, SQL-based tools are evolving to allow querying of data stored in a variety of formats, such as **JSON** and **Parquet**.

SQL in Data Lakes:

- **SQL engines for data lakes**: Tools like **Presto** and **Apache Drill** allow you to run SQL queries directly on data stored in data lakes, regardless of the format.

- **Schema-on-read**: SQL in data lakes often follows a schema-on-read approach, allowing flexibility in how data is queried without requiring predefined schemas.

---

## The Importance of Mastering SQL for Future Data Science Projects

As we move towards a more **data-driven** world, **SQL remains an essential skill** for any data scientist. Mastering SQL opens the door to working efficiently with both small and large datasets, as well as integrating with emerging technologies in cloud computing, machine learning, and big data.

*Why Master SQL for Data Science:*

- **Data wrangling and preparation**: A significant portion of data science involves preparing data for analysis, and SQL is the go-to tool for this task.
- **Integration with machine learning workflows**: SQL is increasingly being integrated into machine learning workflows, making it essential for data scientists working in this field.
- **Working with large-scale data**: With the rise of big data, SQL's role in managing and querying massive datasets is becoming even more important.

- **Cloud and distributed databases**: SQL is central to querying and managing cloud-based data warehouses and distributed databases, which are key for handling big data.

Data scientists who are proficient in SQL will be better positioned to work across all stages of the data pipeline—from data extraction and cleaning to machine learning and reporting.

## Final Thoughts on Becoming an Expert SQL User in Data Science

Becoming an expert SQL user in data science is a continual process of learning and adaptation. As the field evolves, so does SQL's role in data analysis, machine learning, and big data. To truly master SQL, it's important to:

- **Stay updated with new features**: SQL continues to evolve, with new features and functions being added to major databases and platforms. Regularly learning about these changes will keep you ahead of the curve.
- **Focus on optimization**: As data grows, performance becomes crucial. Understanding how to write optimized queries will make you a more efficient data scientist.
- **Integrate SQL with emerging technologies**: SQL's integration with cloud platforms, big data tools, and machine

learning frameworks is increasingly important. Mastering these integrations will give you an edge in your projects.

Mastering SQL in the context of data science not only improves your ability to manipulate and analyze data but also ensures that you are prepared for the future, where data is increasingly complex and voluminous.

---

SQL continues to evolve as an essential tool for **data science** and will remain at the core of querying, data preparation, and analysis. With the rise of **cloud computing**, **big data**, and **machine learning**, SQL is adapting and growing, offering more capabilities to handle large-scale datasets and integrate with new technologies. Mastering SQL is crucial for anyone working in data science, and this chapter has explored the key trends shaping the future of SQL, including:

- **SQL's evolving role** in cloud computing and machine learning.
- **Optimization techniques** for big data.
- The **importance of mastering SQL** to work with future data science projects.

As the landscape of data science continues to change, becoming an expert SQL user will empower you to adapt to new technologies and tackle the complex challenges of the future. The next chapter will focus on **SQL for Advanced Data Science Workflows**, exploring more advanced topics and techniques for leveraging SQL in cutting-edge data science applications.

www.ingramcontent.com/pod-product-compliance
Lightning Source LLC
LaVergne TN
LVHW051436050326
832903LV00030BD/3107